The Book of Arcane Knowledge

500 English Facts for the Curious Mind

F. J. Patterson

THE BOOK OF ARCANE KNOWLEDGE

500 English FACTS FOR THE CURIOUS MIND

By

F. J. Patterson

ARCANE KNOWLEDGE

Arcane knowledge refers to specialized, mysterious, or hidden information, often reserved for those with the insight and expertise to unlock its secrets. The word "arcane" comes from the Latin *arcanus*, meaning "secret" or "hidden," and its first use in English dates back to the late 16th century. Historically, arcane knowledge was tied to ancient practices like alchemy, astrology, and mystical traditions, carefully guarded by scholars, priests, or secret societies. This knowledge was considered esoteric, beyond the grasp of the general public.

As time has passed, the concept of arcane knowledge has evolved, expanding to include a vast range of advanced fields of study. Today, it encompasses the hidden wonders of astronomy, the complexities of genetics and biochemistry, the subtle forces of physics and chemistry, and the intricate workings of evolution and life itself. Yet, it doesn't stop there. History, mathematics, and even language arts like English also form part of this arcane web, where deeper insights into human civilization, the structures of logic, and the power of words lie waiting to be discovered.

Are you ready to open the door?

To Amanda, B a teacher who went above and beyond. Your unwavering dedication and compassion reached beyond any classroom. Thank you for your kindness, patience, and unwavering support, especially when you taught me not just in classrooms but hospital rooms. Thank you for seeing me, for your patience, and for showing me that learning and kindness can thrive even in the toughest places. Your time, effort, and belief in me left an impact I carry with me always.

TABLE OF CONTENTS

TABLE OF CONTENTS

CHAPTER ONE

THE WRITING PROCESS

TRUST
* the *
PROCESS

This chapter outlines key stages in writing: prewriting, drafting, revising, and editing. It introduces techniques like brainstorming and outlining to organize ideas, guides readers on drafting with flow and clarity, and emphasizes revision and editing to polish the final piece. Insights from famous writers illustrate how to turn ideas into well-crafted work.

Prewriting is crucial for organizing thoughts before drafting, helping writers structure their ideas clearly.

Brainstorming allows writers to generate a wide array of ideas, as used by J.K. Rowling when developing the Harry Potter series.

Free writing, a method employed by Ray Bradbury, encourages writers to write continuously without editing to unlock creativity.

Mind mapping helps visualize relationships between ideas; Sylvia Plath used mind mapping to organize themes in her poetry.

Outlining is a strategy Stephen King employs to keep his narratives on track, especially for longer works.

Research is often a vital part of prewriting, as seen in George Orwell's work, where he meticulously gathered information before writing *1984*.

Clustering is a technique that helps create connections between ideas; this was used by John Steinbeck to develop character arcs in *The Grapes of Wrath*.

Writers like Ernest Hemingway often used character sketches in the prewriting phase to develop detailed, realistic characters.

Setting goals for writing can prevent writer's block; Haruki Murakami sets daily word count goals during his prewriting process.

Thesis statements are crafted early to guide argumentative essays, as seen in the works of Malcolm Gladwell, who builds his essays around a clear, central idea.

Drafting is where ideas turn into full sentences and paragraphs; Harper Lee rewrote *To Kill a Mockingbird* multiple times before publication.

During drafting, the goal is to focus on content, not perfection, a method used by Stephen King in his prolific writing.

Ernest Hemingway believed in drafting with purpose, keeping his writing clear and concise through multiple drafts.

Flow in drafting is key, as writers like Virginia Woolf wrote stream-of-consciousness drafts to maintain narrative momentum.

Multiple drafts are common; William Faulkner revised his works several times to enhance his narratives.

Dialogue often begins to form during drafting, with Tennessee Williams famously writing detailed, engaging dialogue for his plays early in the process.

Drafting helps clarify complex ideas, as seen in Ayn Rand's work, where philosophical concepts were broken down into accessible narratives.

Setting and tone are often established in early drafts, as in F. Scott Fitzgerald's *The Great Gatsby*, where tone shaped the entire novel.

Introduction and conclusion paragraphs are vital in essays, often drafted with care to make an impact, as taught by essayists like Joan Didion.

Drafting involves crafting coherent paragraphs, something George Orwell excelled at by structuring his arguments logically.

Revising involves reworking content to improve clarity and structure; Kurt Vonnegut was known for constantly revising his works until satisfied.

Ernest Hemingway is famous for his rigorous revision process, often cutting large sections of text to focus on brevity and precision.

Revising focuses on improving ideas and flow, while editing deals with fixing grammar and punctuation; Jane Austen was meticulous in revising dialogue.

A key part of revision is rearranging sections, a strategy used by James Joyce, who reordered whole chapters in *Ulysses*.

Writers like Ernest Hemingway often revise to eliminate redundancy, cutting unnecessary words to keep sentences sharp.

Peer review during revision can offer new perspectives; Zadie Smith often seeks feedback from peers to refine her work.

Cutting down word count while maintaining meaning is crucial; Mark Twain once said, "I didn't have time to write a short letter, so I wrote a long one."

Writers add transitions during revision to improve flow; J.D. Salinger revised *The Catcher in the Rye* to create smoother shifts between scenes.

Vivid descriptions are often enhanced in revision; Gabriel García Márquez was known for perfecting his imagery during revisions.

Clarity and precision are the primary goals of revision; George Orwell famously aimed to make his prose as clear as possible, believing that unclear writing was tied to unclear thinking.

Editing focuses on mechanics like grammar, spelling, and punctuation; F. Scott Fitzgerald worked tirelessly to perfect his sentence structure in *The Great Gatsby*.

Writers like Anne Lamott recommend reading the text out loud during editing to catch awkward phrasing or errors.

Editing checklists are useful tools, a strategy used by writers like C.S. Lewis to ensure they address all common mistakes.

Ernest Hemingway was a master of concise, clean sentences, and his editing process involved removing excess words to maintain clarity.

Modern writers like Margaret Atwood use editing software to catch minor errors but always manually proofread for deeper issues.

Proofreading is a critical last step, something Agatha Christie emphasized to avoid small mistakes that could confuse readers.

Consistency in tense, tone, and point of view is key in editing; George R.R. Martin ensures continuity across the vast world of *A Song of Ice and Fire*.

Style and format editing is important, especially for academic writing, where authors like Noam Chomsky carefully adhere to style guidelines.

Editing in rounds is a common practice; J.K. Rowling edits for plot consistency first, followed by grammar and sentence structure in later rounds.

Final polish ensures a professional result; Ernest Hemingway famously said, "The only kind of writing is rewriting," emphasizing the importance of thorough editing before publishing.

CHAPTER 2

GRAMMAR AND SENTENCE STRUCTURE

This chapter explores the essential elements of grammar and sentence structure, emphasizing their role in ensuring clarity and precision, much like Jane Austen's refined language. It covers key concepts such as parts of speech, sentence types, punctuation, and subject-verb agreement, demonstrating how careful grammar enhances communication and meaning.

Nouns are words that name a person, place, thing, or idea (e.g., "book," "freedom").

Verbs express actions or states of being (e.g., "run," "is").

Pronouns replace nouns to avoid repetition (e.g., "he," "they").

Adjectives describe or modify nouns (e.g., "beautiful," "fast").

Adverbs modify verbs, adjectives, or other adverbs, often ending in "-ly" (e.g., "quickly," "very").

Prepositions show relationships between nouns or pronouns and other words in a sentence (e.g., "in," "on").

Conjunctions connect words, phrases, or clauses (e.g., "and," "but," "or").

Interjections express strong emotions or sudden reactions (e.g., "Wow!," "Oh!").

Jane Austen used precise grammar to ensure clarity in dialogue, especially in conveying social norms through language.

Determiners (e.g., "the," "a") introduce nouns and specify them (e.g., "the house").

A simple sentence consists of one independent clause (e.g., "Jane writes.").

A compound sentence combines two independent clauses with a coordinating conjunction (e.g., "Jane writes, and she edits.").

A complex sentence consists of an independent clause and one or more dependent clauses (e.g., "Jane writes because she enjoys it.").

Compound-complex sentences include two or more independent clauses and one or more dependent clauses (e.g., "Jane writes, and she edits because she enjoys it.").

Coordinating conjunctions (FANBOYS: For, And, Nor, But, Or, Yet, So) connect clauses in compound sentences.

Subordinating conjunctions (e.g., "because," "although") introduce dependent clauses in complex sentences.

Sentence fragments lack a subject, verb, or complete thought (e.g., "Running down the street."), and should be avoided in formal writing.

Run-on sentences occur when two independent clauses are improperly joined without punctuation or conjunctions.

Jane Austen's use of complex sentences adds depth to her writing, allowing for detailed character insights.

Parallel structure in sentences ensures that elements are balanced (e.g., "She enjoys reading, writing, and editing.").

Periods (.) end declarative sentences and indicate the completion of a thought.

Question marks (?) signal a direct question (e.g., "What time is it?").

Exclamation points (!) indicate strong emotion or emphasis (e.g., "Stop!").

Commas (,) separate elements in a sentence, such as items in a list or clauses (e.g., "She writes, edits, and publishes.").

Semicolons (;) link closely related independent clauses or separate items in a complex list (e.g., "She writes books; he edits articles.").

Colons (:) introduce a list, quote, or explanation (e.g., "She has three goals: write, edit, and publish.").

Apostrophes (') show possession (e.g., "Jane's book") or form contractions (e.g., "don't" for "do not").

Quotation marks (" ") enclose direct speech or quotes (e.g., "Jane said, 'I love writing.'").

Parentheses (()) add extra information or clarification without interrupting the main sentence (e.g., "She published three books (all bestsellers) last year.").

Dashes (—) provide emphasis or indicate an abrupt change in thought (e.g., "I finished my book—finally!").

In subject-verb agreement, singular subjects take singular verbs, and plural subjects take plural verbs (e.g., "The dog runs," "The dogs run").

Collective nouns (e.g., "team," "group") take singular verbs when acting as a single unit (e.g., "The team wins").

Indefinite pronouns like "everyone," "someone," and "nobody" are singular and take singular verbs (e.g., "Everyone is here").

Compound subjects joined by "and" take plural verbs (e.g., "Jane and Tom write"), while those joined by "or" or "nor" agree with the closer subject (e.g., "Neither Jane nor Tom writes").

Inverted sentences (where the verb comes before the subject) still follow subject-verb agreement (e.g., "There are books on the shelf").

Intervening phrases or clauses between the subject and verb do not affect agreement (e.g., "The cake, despite the decorations, tastes good").

Jane Austen's precise use of subject-verb agreement adds to the elegance and clarity of her prose.

When a sentence has a compound subject with singular and plural nouns, the verb agrees with the noun closest to it (e.g., "Either the students or the teacher is going").

Verb tenses should remain consistent throughout a sentence unless there’s a clear reason to change (e.g., "She writes every day but didn’t write yesterday" maintains clarity).

Agreement in complex sentences requires attention to both independent and dependent clauses to ensure grammatical consistency.

CHAPTER 3

VOCABULARY DEVELOPMENT

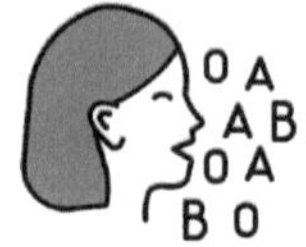

This chapter presents effective vocabulary-building techniques inspired by Shakespeare's innovations in language. Readers learn to use context clues, synonyms, antonyms, and word origins to understand and expand their vocabulary. By applying these methods, anyone can enhance their language skills, echoing the expressive depth of the Bard's timeless work.

Context clues are hints found within a sentence or paragraph that help readers deduce the meaning of unfamiliar words. For example, in the sentence, "The desolate landscape, barren and empty, stretched out for miles," the phrase "barren and empty" helps the reader understand that "desolate" refers to something bleak and uninhabited. Writers use context clues to enhance comprehension without directly defining words.

Definition clues occur when the meaning of an unfamiliar word is explicitly explained within the sentence. For instance, "The arboretum, a place where trees are grown and studied, is open to the public," directly defines "arboretum." This method makes it easy for readers to grasp new vocabulary, a tactic Shakespeare likely used to ensure his audience understood the new words he coined.

Synonym clues provide a familiar word with a similar meaning as the unknown word. For example, "The weather was balmy, warm and pleasant," gives "warm and pleasant" as synonyms for "balmy," helping the reader infer the meaning. Shakespeare used rich synonyms to add variety and depth to his language.

Antonym clues offer a contrasting word to clarify the meaning of an unknown term. In the sentence, "Unlike his jovial nature, today he seemed morose," the word "jovial" gives a clue that "morose" means the opposite—sad or gloomy.

Example clues give specific examples to illustrate the meaning of a word. For example, in "He was an aficionado of outdoor activities, such as hiking, biking, and rock climbing," the examples help define "aficionado" as someone enthusiastic about these activities. Shakespeare often used examples to build complex images and help his audience understand new terms.

Inference clues require the reader to use reasoning to deduce the meaning of an unfamiliar word. For instance, "She gave a curt nod, clearly irritated by the delay," suggests that "curt" means short or abrupt based on the context of irritation.

Restatement clues occur when the meaning of a word is restated in simpler terms within the sentence. For example, "Her demeanor was calm and composed, in other words, tranquil," uses "calm and composed" to clarify that "tranquil" also means peaceful.

Comparison clues involve similes or metaphors to help clarify an unknown word. For example, "The dessert was decadent, just like the rich, creamy cake we had last week," uses comparison to make the meaning of "decadent" more understandable by relating it to something familiar.

Cause-and-effect clues show relationships between ideas to define an unknown word. For instance, "She was famished after skipping lunch, so she devoured the meal quickly," suggests that "famished" means extremely hungry, given the effect of devouring food.

Word roots form the foundation of many words, often from Latin or Greek. For instance, the Latin root "scrib" means "to write," as in "describe" and "manuscript." Shakespeare's knowledge of Latin and Greek roots allowed him to craft new words that felt meaningful.

Prefixes change the meaning of a word when added to the beginning. For example, "pre-" means "before," as in "preview" or "preheat." Shakespeare often manipulated prefixes to invent words like "unreal," using "un-" to mean "not."

Suffixes are added to the end of words to change function or meaning, such as adding "-ful" to "joy" to create "joyful." Shakespeare frequently used suffixes to modify existing words, making English more expressive.

Learning prefixes and suffixes can help readers quickly determine the meanings of new words. For example, the prefix "re-" means "again" or "back," as in "redo" (do again) or "retrace" (go back over steps). The suffix "-tion" turns verbs into nouns, such as "create" becoming "creation."

Latin and Greek roots appear in many English words, like "dict" (Latin for "say" or "speak") in "dictate" and "predict," and "bio" (Greek for "life") in "biology." Shakespeare used classical roots to invent understandable words with familiar origins.

Synonyms are words with similar meanings, like "happy" and "joyful." Expanding vocabulary by learning synonyms allows for precise expression and avoiding repetition. Shakespeare relied on his vast knowledge of synonyms to enrich his plays and add depth.

Antonyms are words with opposite meanings, like "hot" and "cold." Knowing antonyms helps add depth by contrasting ideas or emotions, which Shakespeare used to create tension or highlight differences.

Homonyms are words that sound the same but have different meanings, such as "bare" (uncovered) and "bear" (the animal). Understanding homonyms helps prevent confusion. Shakespeare often used homonyms in puns, adding layers of meaning and humor.

Homophones sound alike but are spelled differently, like "their," "there," and "they're." Shakespeare's audience enjoyed his clever use of homophones in puns.

Etymology is the study of a word's history and evolution. Knowing etymology deepens appreciation for language, something Shakespeare was well-versed in, often deriving words from Latin and Greek.

A thesaurus helps writers find synonyms and expand vocabulary. It allows writers to discover new words to express ideas more effectively, which is something Shakespeare likely used or relied on in an equivalent way.

William Shakespeare's use of synonyms, antonyms, and inventive vocabulary helped shape the English language. His mastery of language allowed him to express complex human emotions with clarity and depth.

CHAPTER 4

CRITICAL READING AND COMPREHENSION

This chapter focuses on close reading strategies for analyzing both nonfiction and fiction texts, with an emphasis on identifying bias and evaluating arguments. Inspired by George Orwell's works, such as *1984* and *Animal Farm*, it highlights the importance of critical analysis in understanding complex texts.

Close reading involves analyzing a text carefully, focusing on every detail to uncover deeper meanings, especially in complex works like George Orwell's *1984*.

Annotation is a technique where readers highlight key passages and make notes, engaging with the text as Orwell's readers do to better understand his social and political commentary.

Identifying key themes helps reveal a text's deeper meanings. Orwell's *Animal Farm* uses allegory and symbolism to explore themes like power and corruption.

Examining the structure of a text can uncover how the author builds their argument or story. In *1984*, Orwell's structure mirrors the oppressive nature of the regime.

Identifying patterns, such as repeated phrases or imagery, shows connections between ideas.

Orwell's paradoxical slogans in *1984*, like "War is Peace," reinforce the regime’s control over thought.

Language choices are vital. Orwell's *Newspeak* in *1984* serves as a tool of control, highlighting linguistic manipulation in totalitarian regimes.

Tone and mood reveal a text's emotional impact. Orwell's consistently grim tone in *1984* reflects the oppressive environment he describes.

Identifying the author's purpose is key to close reading. Orwell’s use of allegory in *Animal Farm* critiques the Soviet Union’s betrayal of the socialist revolution.

Considering historical context is crucial for understanding Orwell’s works, influenced by the political climate of the 20th century, particularly the Russian Revolution and Stalinism.

Recognizing allusions enhances comprehension. Orwell’s frequent references to historical events and ideologies deepen the meaning of his work.

Fiction texts, like *1984*, are analyzed for narrative techniques such as plot, character development, and symbolism, whereas **nonfiction** focuses on the author's argument, evidence, and purpose.

Character analysis in fiction reveals how characters develop and reflect larger themes. In *1984*, Winston Smith’s evolution shows how a totalitarian regime erodes individuality.

Setting analysis helps understand larger themes, like the bleak environment in *1984*, which symbolizes the Party's crushing power.

Theme analysis uncovers central messages, such as the corruption of power in *Animal Farm*, which mirrors Stalinist Russia.

Evaluating arguments in nonfiction involves assessing the evidence behind claims, as seen in Orwell's political essays, where his arguments are supported by historical examples.

Plot structure in fiction builds tension, as in *1984*, where Winston's rebellion culminates in a tragic climax, emphasizing the hopelessness of resistance in a totalitarian state.

Identifying bias requires detecting the author's perspective. Orwell's works, like *Animal Farm*, critique totalitarian regimes, revealing his political bias.

Authorial bias shapes how information is presented, such as Orwell's portrayal of Stalinist Russia in *Animal Farm*.

Evaluating arguments requires assessing logic and evidence. Orwell's essays often use historical examples to strengthen his critiques of totalitarianism.

Detecting logical fallacies helps readers understand manipulation. Orwell exposes the Party's use of contradictory slogans in *1984*, revealing the dangers of flawed logic.

Subtle bias can be found in language choices, as in Orwell's portrayal of Napoleon in *Animal Farm*, which reflects his disapproval of Stalinist leadership.

Identifying counterarguments strengthens analysis, as Orwell often addresses opposing views in his essays, adding depth to his arguments.

Cultural and historical bias affects interpretation. Orwell's experiences with British imperialism and totalitarian regimes influence his critiques in both fiction and nonfiction.

Recognizing emotional appeals is crucial. Orwell uses emotional language in *1984* to evoke fear and highlight the horrors of totalitarianism.

Fact-checking ensures the accuracy of nonfiction texts. Orwell's claims in his essays should be cross-referenced with historical facts for validation.

Propaganda is central in Orwell's works, particularly *1984*, where the Party manipulates truth through controlling information, a critique of government propaganda.

Skimming and scanning are useful for identifying key points quickly.

Summarizing the text helps solidify understanding, as with *Animal Farm*, where summarizing the pigs' rise and fall highlights themes of power and corruption.

Asking questions while reading deepens comprehension, like analyzing Orwell’s use of irony in *1984*.

Making connections between the text and personal experiences enhances understanding, as Orwell’s critique of surveillance in *1984* resonates with modern concerns.

Paraphrasing difficult passages can clarify meanings, especially in Orwell's dense political commentary.

Breaking down long sentences aids in understanding complex ideas.

Visualizing the text brings abstract ideas to life, such as picturing Winston's experience in *1984*.

Rereading difficult sections reveals new insights, often uncovering nuances in Orwell's work.

Creating outlines of key points helps clarify the text's structure and arguments, particularly in nonfiction essays.

Discussion and debate enrich understanding, encouraging deeper exploration of themes like power, freedom, and control in *1984*.

CHAPTER 5

LITERARY DEVICES AND FIGURATIVE LANGUAGE

This chapter explores the key literary devices in *The Great Gatsby* and how they shape the novel's themes, character depth, and emotional impact. Through elements like symbolism, foreshadowing, and metaphor, F. Scott Fitzgerald's storytelling reveals complex layers, deepening the portrayal of the American Dream, love, and identity. This breakdown offers readers a fresh perspective on how Fitzgerald's language and style bring the story to life.

Metaphors compare two unlike things without using "like" or "as." Fitzgerald often uses metaphors to convey deeper meanings, like describing Gatsby's dream as a "green light," symbolizing hope and unattainable desires.

Personification gives human qualities to non-human objects or ideas. Fitzgerald personifies elements of the environment, like the "restless" water of the bay, mirroring the characters' emotional states.

Similes create vivid imagery that helps readers visualize the text. Fitzgerald frequently compares characters to objects or animals to convey traits or emotions in a relatable way.

Metaphors add layers of meaning to the narrative. The "valley of ashes" represents moral decay and hopelessness beneath the wealthy class's surface in *The Great Gatsby.*

Personification breathes life into inanimate elements, making the text more dynamic.

Fitzgerald's personification of the landscape around Gatsby's mansion reflects Gatsby's grandeur and mystery.

Similes can express emotions indirectly. When Fitzgerald writes that Tom Buchanan's voice is "as harsh as a whip," it evokes the character's cruel and controlling nature.

Metaphors can reflect themes in a novel. The green light symbolizes Gatsby's impossible dream and the broader illusion of the American Dream.

Personification can reflect tone and mood. Fitzgerald describes the "dead dream" to emphasize finality and melancholy in the narrative.

Similes enhance descriptions by creating relatable comparisons. Fitzgerald describes Daisy's voice as "full of money," emphasizing her association with wealth.

Symbolism is when objects, characters, or events represent something deeper. The green light at Daisy's dock symbolizes Gatsby's unattainable dream.

Foreshadowing hints at future events in a narrative. Fitzgerald uses foreshadowing to build suspense, like when weather mirrors emotional tones, foreshadowing Gatsby's death.

Irony involves a contrast between expectations and reality. For example, Gatsby's lavish parties, intended to win Daisy, ultimately repel her.

Irony adds depth to characters and themes. Gatsby's wealth fails to bring happiness, highlighting the American Dream's ironic nature.

Symbolism creates layers of meaning. The valley of ashes symbolizes the divide between wealth and poverty and the moral decay of the rich.

Foreshadowing can be subtle or direct. Myrtle's tragic end is foreshadowed by her reckless behavior and obsession with wealth.

Irony can create social commentary. Fitzgerald criticizes the upper class's shallow nature, as characters feign care but are ultimately self-serving.

Symbolism is open to interpretation. The green light symbolizes Gatsby's dream and the broader theme of human ambition.

Imagery uses descriptive language to create vivid mental pictures. Fitzgerald's descriptions of Gatsby's lavish parties evoke the Jazz Age's excess.

Hyperbole is a deliberate exaggeration for emphasis. Fitzgerald uses hyperbole to highlight Gatsby's wealth, describing his car as "a rich cream color, bright with nickel."

Onomatopoeia imitates sounds. Fitzgerald uses onomatopoeia subtly, like the "chug-chug" of Gatsby's boat, adding realism to scenes.

Imagery engages the senses. Fitzgerald's "blue gardens" filled with the sound of "oboes and trombones" immerse readers in Gatsby's world.

Hyperbole can emphasize characters' traits. Nick's description of Gatsby's "smile of eternal reassurance" exaggerates Gatsby's charisma.

Onomatopoeia adds realism. Words like "buzzing" or "humming" in party scenes give a sensory experience of the lively atmosphere.

Imagery can reflect themes. Describing Daisy's voice as "full of money" highlights the theme of wealth and materialism.

Hyperbole enhances emotional impact. Fitzgerald's description of Gatsby's lifestyle emphasizes his obsession with impressing Daisy.

Onomatopoeia can create mood. The "soft murmur" at Gatsby's parties contrasts with "loud crash" accidents, symbolizing fragility and impending doom.

Imagery can evoke symbolism. The green light's glow across the bay symbolizes Gatsby's unreachable dreams and distance from Daisy.

Metaphors contribute to themes. Describing Gatsby as a "son of God" emphasizes his self-made persona and obsession with the American Dream.

Symbolism conveys moral lessons. Cars and accidents in *The Great Gatsby* symbolize characters' recklessness and its fatal consequences.

Foreshadowing often involves imagery. Darkening skies and stormy weather foreshadow Gatsby's demise, using natural imagery to signal doom.

Hyperbole can critique lifestyles. In *The Great Gatsby*, hyperbole showcases the wealthy's excesses and shallow pursuits.

Personification gives objects emotional significance. Describing Gatsby's house as "lonely" reflects his isolation despite outward success.

Irony reveals deeper truths. Gatsby's tragic end critiques the futility of the American Dream, showing that wealth does not guarantee happiness.

Imagery can shift tone. As *The Great Gatsby* progresses, imagery shifts from lively to somber, reflecting the mood change from optimism to tragedy.

Foreshadowing and **symbolism** often overlap. Fitzgerald's description of the "foul dust" following Gatsby's dreams foreshadows his inevitable failure.

Irony highlights hypocrisy. Characters who condemn others are often guilty of similar behavior, critiquing the wealthy's moral hypocrisy.

Imagery encapsulates themes. The "fresh, green breast of the new world" symbolizes lost dreams, linking themes of ambition and disillusionment to the American experience.

CHAPTER 6

ANALYZING THEMES IN LITERATURE

This chapter explores how literary devices shape key themes like justice, identity, and empathy in *To Kill a Mockingbird.* Inspired by Harper Lee's novel, we examine symbolism, irony, and imagery to see how they bring the story's moral and social messages to life. Symbolism—like the mockingbird itself—reflects themes of innocence and prejudice, while irony and foreshadowing expose moral contradictions and hint at underlying tensions. Through these techniques, Lee creates a vivid portrayal of societal injustices, fostering empathy and challenging readers to consider the impact of compassion and integrity in confronting prejudice.

Themes are the central ideas or messages an author explores throughout a literary work. For example, in *To Kill a Mockingbird*, Harper Lee explores racial injustice, morality, and compassion.

Love is a common theme in literature, often depicted through relationships between characters. In *To Kill a Mockingbird*, the love between family members, particularly Atticus Finch and his children, forms the story's emotional core.

Power as a theme can manifest in different forms, such as societal, political, or personal power. Harper Lee addresses the power dynamics between races, especially how those in power maintain control through prejudice.

Identity is frequently explored as a theme, focusing on how characters understand themselves and others. Scout Finch's journey of self-discovery in *To Kill a Mockingbird* highlights how experiences and social environment shape identity.

Themes can be universal—meaning they apply to people and societies across different times and cultures. The theme of justice in *To Kill a Mockingbird* is universally relevant as societies worldwide grapple with issues of fairness and morality.

Authors use characters to represent different sides of a theme. In *To Kill a Mockingbird,* Atticus Finch represents moral courage and integrity, while characters like Bob Ewell represent hatred and prejudice.

Themes of love can be complicated, exploring different types such as familial, romantic, or platonic love. In *To Kill a Mockingbird*, Harper Lee explores the love Atticus has for his children, teaching them life's most difficult lessons.

Themes of power often explore how characters gain, lose, or abuse power. In *To Kill a Mockingbird*, the court system and Tom Robinson's trial reflect the abuse of power by those who control the legal system.

Identity themes are central to the character of Scout Finch, who grows up in a racially divided town and learns to navigate her beliefs in a world filled with prejudice and stereotypes.

Love and sacrifice can be interwoven themes. Atticus sacrifices his reputation and personal safety in defending Tom Robinson, showing the depth of his love for justice and morality.

Themes develop through the actions of characters. In *To Kill a Mockingbird*, Atticus' decision to defend Tom Robinson is pivotal to developing the theme of racial injustice.

Plots often revolve around key events that help to highlight a theme. The trial of Tom Robinson in *To Kill a Mockingbird*is central to developing the theme of the legal system's failure to protect innocent people based on race.

Characters evolve to reflect the themes. Scout Finch's understanding of good and evil evolves throughout *To Kill a Mockingbird*, highlighting the theme of innocence lost in the face of real-world complexities.

Themes of conflict between characters can underscore broader societal issues. The tension between Atticus Finch and the townspeople reflects the broader racial conflict in Maycomb, developing the theme of moral integrity versus societal expectations.

Themes can deepen as the plot progresses. In *To Kill a Mockingbird*, the theme of justice becomes more nuanced as Scout learns that justice is not always served in the court of law.

Dialogue between characters can reveal thematic elements. Atticus' conversations with

Scout and Jem about racism and empathy highlight the theme of moral education.

Character decisions drive thematic development. Atticus' choice to defend Tom Robinson at significant personal risk illustrates the theme of standing up for what is right, even when it's unpopular.

Character arcs often reflect the development of a theme. Jem Finch's journey from innocence to disillusionment mirrors the theme of growing up and facing harsh realities about human nature and society.

Subplots often reinforce the main theme. The subplot of Boo Radley's mysterious presence in the novel develops the theme of prejudice, as the children's initial fear of him gives way to understanding and compassion.

Themes can contrast with one another, providing complexity to the narrative. In *To Kill a Mockingbird*, the harsh realities of prejudice and injustice constantly challenge the theme of innocence.

Conflict is central to theme development. The conflict between Atticus Finch and the racist townspeople drives the theme of standing up against prejudice.

Internal conflicts within characters can highlight themes. Scout's internal struggle with understanding good versus evil develops the theme of moral growth and innocence.

External conflicts between characters or society drive the plot and reinforce themes. Tom Robinson's trial reflects the external conflict between individual rights and systemic racism.

Conflict resolution in a story can convey the author's stance on the theme. In *To Kill a Mockingbird*, the lack of justice for Tom Robinson reflects the harsh truth of racial inequality, a theme that Harper Lee emphasizes through the trial's outcome.

Not all conflicts are resolved, which can reinforce the theme. Tom Robinson's death underscores the theme of injustice, as even Atticus Finch's best efforts could not save him from a discriminatory system.

Character-driven conflict helps clarify themes. The conflict between Atticus and Bob Ewell highlights the theme of integrity versus hatred, with Atticus representing moral strength.

The resolution of conflict can be positive or negative. The lack of justice in Tom Robinson's trial represents a negative resolution that reinforces the novel's theme of societal failure in addressing racial inequality.

Themes evolve as conflicts are introduced. The introduction of racial conflict through Tom Robinson's trial expands the theme of justice beyond the family dynamic into a broader societal context.

Conflicts involving social structures like the court system develop themes related to power and oppression. In *To Kill a Mockingbird*, the legal system's failure to deliver justice for Tom Robinson highlights systemic racism.

The resolution of minor conflicts can symbolize thematic resolutions. Boo Radley saving Scout and Jem resolves the theme of fear and misunderstanding, showing that people are often not what society assumes them to be.

Harper Lee uses symbolism to support the development of her themes. The mockingbird symbolizes innocence, and those who harm it, like Tom Robinson and Boo Radley, face undeserved punishment.

The theme of empathy is explored through Atticus Finch's advice to Scout about understanding others by walking in their shoes.

This lesson becomes central to Scout's moral development.

Justice versus injustice is a dominant theme. The failure of the court system to protect Tom Robinson represents the larger societal theme of racial injustice and the need for reform.

Harper Lee contrasts childhood innocence with adult prejudice, showing how society's values can corrupt innocence over time, as Scout's growing awareness of racism shows.

Themes can be timeless and applicable to different historical periods. Although *To Kill a Mockingbird* was set during the Great Depression, its themes of racial injustice and moral integrity remain relevant today.

Atticus Finch embodies the theme of moral courage, standing up for justice in the face of overwhelming social opposition. His character serves as a role model for integrity and empathy.

The themes of good versus evil are explored through the characters' moral choices. While Bob Ewell represents evil, characters like Atticus and Miss Maudie stand for good, showing the novel's moral complexities.

Themes of social inequality are evident in the town's rigid class system. In addition to racial prejudice, Harper Lee explores economic and gender inequalities in the community.

Resolution of the thematic conflict of understanding others occurs when Scout stands on Boo Radley's porch, realizing that he was a protector, not a monster, fulfilling Atticus' lesson about empathy.

CHAPTER 7

LITERARY ANALYSIS

This chapter guides students through literary analysis using Nathaniel Hawthorne's *The Scarlet Letter*. Focusing on key techniques, devices, and themes, students will explore how Hawthorne's complex characters and powerful symbolism convey deeper meanings. By analyzing characters like Hester Prynne and Arthur Dimmesdale, as well as symbols like the scarlet letter, students will learn how to interpret and evaluate the moral and psychological layers of the novel.

Definition and Purpose Literary analysis is the art of delving deeply into a literary work to uncover its underlying themes, symbols, and messages. It involves interpreting the author's intentions and how they are expressed through techniques like narrative structure, character development, and language. This practice enhances appreciation of literature by revealing the intricate layers that contribute to its meaning.

Thesis Statement as a Foundation
A strong literary analysis hinges on a thesis statement that guides the entire argument. For instance, in analyzing *The Scarlet Letter*, one might argue: "Hawthorne critiques Puritanical hypocrisy by juxtaposing Hester's dignity in accepting her sin with Dimmesdale's tormented secrecy." This serves as the analysis's focal point.

Specificity and Argument in Thesis Statements An effective thesis is both specific and arguable, providing a clear lens for examining the text. For example, rather than stating, "Hawthorne uses symbolism," a stronger thesis would assert, "Through the evolving meaning of the scarlet letter 'A,' Hawthorne critiques societal transformation and resilience in the face of stigma."

Importance of Close Reading Close reading emphasizes how a text conveys meaning. Analyzing Hawthorne's description of the scarlet letter's embroidery reveals Hester's agency: despite her punishment, she reclaims the symbol as a form of self-expression.

Role of Textual Evidence Literary analysis thrives on evidence. Quotes like "On the breast of her gown, in fine red cloth, surrounded with an elaborate embroidery and fantastic flourishes of gold thread" exemplify how Hester transforms the symbol of her shame into artful defiance.

Adding Context Historical, cultural, or biographical context enriches understanding.

Knowing Hawthorne's Puritan ancestry, for example, reveals his ambivalence toward their moral rigidity, making *The Scarlet Letter* both a critique and a reflection of his heritage.

Breaking Down the Text Understanding a literary work requires dissecting its elements—plot, characters, setting, and themes. Each component functions like a puzzle piece, contributing to the overall narrative and thematic picture.

Difference Between Summary and Analysis While summary recounts the what, analysis explores the why and how. For instance, summarizing Hester's ostracism misses the opportunity to analyze how her resilience challenges societal norms.

Logical Organization of Analysis An organized analysis guides readers seamlessly through its argument. An introduction sets the stage, body paragraphs unpack specific evidence, and a conclusion ties back to the thesis while offering deeper insights.

Effective Conclusions A conclusion should synthesize findings, restating the thesis in light of the evidence. In *The Scarlet Letter*, one might conclude that Hawthorne's critique of Puritanism underscores the universal struggle between personal morality and societal judgment.

The Role of Techniques Literary techniques like symbolism, diction, and tone are the foundation of effective storytelling. Authors use these tools intentionally to convey deeper meanings, evoke emotions, and enrich the reader's understanding of the text. Identifying and interpreting these techniques allows readers to engage more fully with a work's complexity and purpose.

Diction as a Window to Meaning
Diction, or word choice, can reveal an author's intent and the text's underlying themes. In *The*

Scarlet Letter, Hawthorne's use of archaic diction—words like ignominy and betokened—not only establishes the historical and cultural setting but also reflects the formal, moralistic tone of Puritan society. This deliberate choice immerses readers in the era and reinforces the novel's gravitas.

Tone in Literary Works Tone reflects the author's attitude toward the subject and characters. Hawthorne's tone in *The Scarlet Letter* is somber yet empathetic. His nuanced portrayal of Hester Prynne, for instance, invites readers to sympathize with her plight while critically examining the harshness of Puritanical values. This duality enhances the novel's moral complexity.

Impact of Point of View The third-person omniscient narration in *The Scarlet Letter* provides a panoramic view of the characters' inner struggles and motivations. By delving into Dimmesdale's concealed guilt, Chillingworth's vengeful obsession, and Hester's resilience,

Hawthorne offers a comprehensive exploration of sin and redemption from multiple perspectives.

Power of Symbolism Symbolism is central to Hawthorne's storytelling. The scarlet letter "A," initially a symbol of shame, transforms over the course of the novel into a mark of strength and individuality. This evolution mirrors Hester's journey from societal condemnation to personal empowerment, showcasing Hawthorne's critique of societal judgment.

Allegorical Layers *The Scarlet Letter* operates as an allegory for the tension between personal truth and societal expectation. Characters like Hester, Dimmesdale, and Chillingworth symbolize broader moral conflicts, such as authenticity versus hypocrisy and forgiveness versus vengeance.

Significance of Setting The setting of Puritan New England is more than a backdrop—it actively shapes the narrative. Its strict codes of morality and public shaming practices drive the plot and underscore the themes of judgment, hypocrisy, and resilience.

Depth Through Characterization
Hawthorne's characters are multidimensional, each embodying moral and psychological complexities. Hester represents strength and redemption, Dimmesdale illustrates hidden guilt and hypocrisy, and Chillingworth epitomizes the destructive power of vengeance. These detailed character studies deepen the novel's themes of sin and forgiveness.

Role of Imagery Hawthorne's use of vivid imagery enhances the emotional and symbolic layers of the story. Dark, shadowy forests symbolize secrecy and sin, while moments of light and openness represent truth and revelation. This imagery reinforces the novel's exploration of concealed versus exposed guilt.

Themes in Literary Analysis Themes are the central ideas explored in a literary work. In *The*

Scarlet Letter, themes like sin, redemption, and societal judgment are intricately woven into the narrative. Analyzing these themes reveals Hawthorne's critique of rigid morality and his exploration of human resilience.

Sin and Redemption Hester Prynne's journey demonstrates the possibility of redemption through dignity and personal strength. Dimmesdale’s contrasting path, marked by hidden guilt and self-punishment, underscores the destructive power of unacknowledged sin. Hawthorne contrasts these two paths to explore how individuals confront their moral failings.

Hypocrisy and Judgment Hawthorne exposes the hypocrisy of a society that condemns Hester while ignoring the sins of others, like Dimmesdale. This theme critiques the tendency of communities to impose strict moral standards while concealing their own flaws.

The Role of Nature Nature in *The Scarlet Letter* serves as a sanctuary for truth and freedom, contrasting with the oppressive Puritan society. The forest scenes, where Hester and Dimmesdale meet away from the prying eyes of the community, symbolize a space where they can express their true selves.

Historical and Cultural Context in Analysis Understanding the historical context of Puritan New England enriches the analysis of *The Scarlet Letter*. The rigid religious framework and emphasis on public punishment reflect societal values that Hawthorne critiques through the characters' experiences.

Irony in Literature Hawthorne employs irony to highlight societal contradictions. For example, the town leaders who enforce morality are often the least moral characters in the novel. Dimmesdale, the revered minister, hides a grave sin, exemplifying the gap between appearance and reality.

Foreshadowing as a Narrative Tool Foreshadowing builds tension and prepares readers for significant events. Early references to Dimmesdale clutching his chest hint at his concealed guilt, which is later revealed to be symbolized by his own version of the scarlet letter.

Metaphors and Extended Analogies

Hawthorne uses metaphors to deepen the reader's understanding of his themes. The scaffold, for instance, represents both public shame and the possibility of redemption. Characters' interactions with the scaffold reflect their personal growth or downfall.

Motifs and Recurring Elements

Recurring motifs, such as light and darkness, emphasize the duality of truth and secrecy. Light often symbolizes revelation, as seen in the moment when Hester's scarlet letter is illuminated in the governor's hall, highlighting her vulnerability.

The Author's Intent Understanding Hawthorne's personal background and intent adds depth to analysis. His Puritan heritage and ambivalence toward its moral strictness inform his sympathetic yet critical portrayal of his characters and their struggles.

Analyzing Dialogue Dialogue reveals characters' personalities, motivations, and conflicts. Dimmesdale's speech patterns, filled with hesitation and self-doubt, contrast with Hester's confident and resolute tone, underscoring their differing responses to sin.

Interpreting Symbols in Context
Symbols often take on different meanings depending on their context within the story. The scarlet letter "A," initially a mark of shame, evolves to symbolize Hester's resilience and individuality, reflecting her growth and the shifting perceptions of those around her.

Psychological Depth in Characters
Hawthorne's exploration of guilt, shame, and revenge provides psychological depth to his characters. Dimmesdale's internal conflict

illustrates the torment of unconfessed sin, while Chillingworth's obsessive pursuit of vengeance highlights the corrosive effects of unchecked hatred.

Impact of Narrative Structure

The non-linear narrative of *The Scarlet Letter*, with its flashbacks and gradual revelations, mirrors the complexity of its themes. This structure allows Hawthorne to explore the consequences of past actions and the evolution of his characters over time.

Synthesis of Evidence

A strong analysis synthesizes evidence to support a coherent argument. For example, one might combine observations about Hester's characterization, the symbolism of the scarlet letter, and the Puritan setting to argue that Hawthorne critiques the rigidity of societal norms while celebrating individual resilience.

Adapting Analysis to Audience

Effective literary analysis considers its

audience. A formal analysis might focus on academic interpretations, while a casual discussion could emphasize relatable themes or personal connections to the text. Tailoring the analysis ensures its relevance and accessibility.

The Role of Criticism in Analysis

Engaging with literary criticism can provide new perspectives. Reading critiques of *The Scarlet Letter* might highlight overlooked themes, such as feminist readings of Hester's defiance or psychoanalytic interpretations of Dimmesdale's guilt.

Conclusion: The Value of Literary Analysis

Literary analysis fosters a deeper appreciation of literature by uncovering its layers of meaning. Through close reading and thoughtful interpretation, works like *The Scarlet Letter* transform from stories into profound explorations of the human condition, challenging readers to reflect on their own lives and societies.

CHAPTER 8

POINT OF VIEW AND PERSPECTIVE

This chapter explores the impact of point of view and perspective, focusing on Edgar Allan Poe's use of unreliable narrators, particularly in *The Tell-Tale Heart*. It examines how narrative perspective shapes readers' perceptions, distorts reality, and deepens psychological tension.

Definition and Role of Point of View (POV): POV is the lens through which a story is told. It shapes the narrative by determining what the reader knows, how they perceive the characters, and how they emotionally engage with the plot. The chosen POV influences the narrative tone, mood, and how much of the world the reader is allowed to access.

First-Person POV: In first-person narration, the story is told from the perspective of a character using "I" or "we." This allows the reader to experience the protagonist's thoughts, emotions, and personal journey in a highly intimate and direct way. However, it limits the narrative to the perceptions and knowledge of that one character, often making the story more subjective. It creates a sense of immediacy but also of bias, as the reader only gets one viewpoint, which can be unreliable depending on the narrator's mental state.

Third-Person Limited POV: The third-person limited point of view uses “he,” “she,” or “they” to tell the story but focuses on one character’s inner thoughts and emotions at a time. This perspective offers a blend of intimacy and objectivity, allowing readers to see a character's inner struggles while still maintaining some distance from their mind. It is particularly effective in building suspense, as it can withhold critical information about other characters, leading to surprises as the story progresses. Third-person limited also helps focus the narrative, keeping the reader aligned with the protagonist’s emotional arc.

Third-Person Omniscient POV: In third-person omniscient narration, the narrator has access to the thoughts, emotions, and experiences of all characters in the story. This “all-knowing” perspective offers a broader and more comprehensive understanding of the narrative, providing insight into subplots and secondary characters. While this allows the reader to see multiple viewpoints, it can sometimes feel detached because the narrator is not bound by the limitations of any single character. The omniscient narrator may describe scenes or characters in ways that characters themselves cannot perceive, creating a god-like distance from the events.

Subjectivity and Bias in First-Person POV: One of the critical aspects of first-person narration is its inherent subjectivity. The reader is limited to the narrator's experiences, emotions, and knowledge, which can lead to a biased interpretation of events. This can make the story feel more personal and emotionally engaging but also unreliable. In Edgar Allan Poe's works, like *The Tell-Tale Heart*, the narrator's insistence on their sanity despite clear signs of madness forces readers to question the accuracy of the narrative, creating a tension between perception and reality.

Focus and Suspense in Third-Person Limited POV: By restricting the narrative to one character's experiences, third-person limited POV creates suspense and intrigue. The reader knows only as much as the protagonist does, which can withhold crucial information about other characters' motivations and secrets. This can generate dramatic irony, where the reader knows something the character does not, amplifying the tension and making the eventual revelation all the more impactful.

Breadth and Objectivity in Third-Person Omniscient POV: The omniscient narrator can shift between characters' thoughts and experiences, offering the reader a comprehensive view of the plot. This broad scope allows the narrator to provide detailed backgrounds, motivations, and subtext that no single character could reveal. However, while it allows for a fuller understanding of the world and the characters, it often sacrifices the emotional intimacy and focus on one character that is more prevalent in first-person or third-person limited narration.

Impact of POV Choice on the Narrative: The choice of POV influences what information is revealed to the reader, how they perceive the characters, and the overall tone of the story. For instance, a first-person perspective can create a personal, emotional connection but may limit the reader's understanding of the broader world or other characters. In contrast, third-person omniscient provides a more complete view of the world but may feel less emotionally charged or personal. Each perspective brings its own strengths and weaknesses to a narrative.

Unreliable Narration in First-Person POV: First-person narrators often present an incomplete or biased version of events. Their perspective is limited to their own experiences, and their emotions can color their interpretation of reality. Edgar Allan Poe frequently employs this technique, particularly in stories like *The Tell-Tale Heart*, where the narrator's desperate attempts to convince the reader of their sanity only highlight their fractured mental state. The unreliability of the first-person narrator challenges readers to question the truth of what they are being told.

The Detachment of Omniscient Narration: Although third-person omniscient narration allows for a comprehensive understanding of the plot and characters, it can sometimes diminish the emotional impact of the story. The distance created by the narrator's god-like perspective can make it difficult for readers to form a strong emotional bond with the characters, particularly when their internal thoughts and experiences are presented alongside those of other characters.

Shaping the Reader's Understanding: Perspective is essential in how readers experience a story. It determines what the reader knows and when they know it, thus controlling the flow of information and emotion. First-person perspectives provide a deep dive into one character's psyche, while third-person limited allows a more controlled exploration of the protagonist's emotions and thoughts. Third-person omniscient offers a panoramic view of the entire world, making it ideal for stories with multiple complex characters and subplots.

Emotional Connection in First-Person POV: First-person narration creates a direct window into the narrator's mind, establishing a deep emotional connection between the reader and the protagonist. Readers experience events through the eyes of the narrator, often feeling their confusion, joy, fear, or sorrow. This emotional depth can make first-person narration particularly compelling, as it allows for an intense, personalized experience of the narrative.

Creating Suspense with Third-Person Limited POV: By focusing on the inner thoughts and experiences of only one character, third-person limited POV can withhold critical information from the reader. This restriction creates a sense of suspense, as readers are only privy to the protagonist's knowledge and perceptions. The unknown motivations and actions of other characters keep the reader on edge, building tension throughout the narrative.

Holistic Understanding in Omniscient POV: Third-person omniscient narration allows for a more holistic understanding of the events unfolding in the story. By accessing the thoughts and experiences of multiple characters, the omniscient narrator can reveal the contrasts between characters' inner lives and their outward actions. This broader view can illuminate the complexity of relationships, motivations, and conflicts within the story.

Shifting Perspectives in Complex Narratives: Many stories, particularly those in the epic or multi-character genre, use shifts in perspective to provide a fuller understanding of the plot. This technique allows authors to explore multiple characters' viewpoints, each offering a different angle on the same events. This multifaceted approach enriches the narrative, providing depth to the characters and plot.

Poe's Use of First-Person Narration: Edgar Allan Poe frequently uses first-person POV to explore the depths of his characters' minds. This approach allows him to delve deeply into themes of paranoia, guilt, and madness. The first-person perspective in stories like *The Tell-Tale Heart* forces the reader to confront the narrator's fractured state of mind, making the story both personal and disturbing.

Psychological Exploration through First-Person: In Poe's works, first-person narration is used not just as a narrative tool but as a means of exploring the psychological breakdown of the protagonist. The reader is given access to the narrator's inner turmoil, making it impossible to separate the events from the narrator's distorted perceptions of reality.

Reliability and Truth: The reliability of the narrator is central to the reader's understanding of the story. In first-person and third-person limited POVs, the narrative is confined to the knowledge and perception of the protagonist. As a result, what the reader knows can be limited, distorted, or incomplete. In stories like *The Tell-Tale Heart* and *The Black Cat*, Poe uses unreliable narrators to blur the line between reality and delusion, leaving the reader to question what is true.

Contrast and Complexity in Omniscient Narration: In third-person omniscient narration, the ability to shift between characters allows for a deeper understanding of the contrasts between their inner thoughts and their outward behavior. This can add complexity to the narrative, as characters' actions may seem contradictory when viewed from different perspectives. The omniscient narrator can show how characters deceive each other and themselves, enriching the story with layers of meaning.

Dramatic Irony and Limited POV: When the narrator knows less than the reader, it can create dramatic irony, a situation where the reader knows something that the character does not. This heightens tension and keeps the audience engaged, as they anticipate the moment when the character discovers the truth.

Unreliable Narrators: An unreliable narrator is one whose version of events is questionable or distorted. This can happen for a variety of reasons, such as mental illness, dishonesty, or selective memory. The reader must critically analyze the narrative, piecing together clues to understand the truth of the story.

Psychological, Bias, and Limited Knowledge: Unreliable narrators often have psychological issues, biases, or limited understanding of events, which makes them unreliable. Their personal agendas or emotional states can color their perception of reality, distorting the truth. This forces the reader to engage more deeply with the text to understand the underlying story.

Poe's Use of Unreliable Narrators: In works like *The Tell-Tale Heart* and *The Black Cat*, Poe uses unreliable narrators to create tension and to explore themes of guilt and insanity. By presenting the story through the eyes of characters who cannot trust their own perceptions, Poe forces the reader to question what is real and what is imagined.

Narrative Bias and Perspective: The bias of the narrator can shape the reader's perception of events. A biased narrator will present a skewed version of reality, leading the reader to form judgments about the characters and events based on incomplete or misleading information. In stories with unreliable narrators, this bias can lead to surprising twists and revelations as the truth emerges.

Narrative Tension and Mystery in First-Person: First-person narration often heightens tension and mystery by limiting what the reader knows. Since the narrative unfolds through the eyes of one character, the reader only gets their personal knowledge, thoughts, and experiences. This sense of mystery can be particularly effective in genres such as thriller, mystery, or horror, where the protagonist's knowledge of their situation is incomplete or unclear. The reader, therefore, experiences the same confusion and uncertainty as the narrator, building suspense and anticipation.

Character Development through First-Person: In first-person POV, readers have direct access to a character's thoughts, motivations, and inner conflicts. This can provide a deep, intimate understanding of the character's development, allowing the audience to witness the changes in the protagonist's psyche. The emotional journey becomes much more tangible, and the reader feels personally connected to the character's growth or struggles. This deep psychological immersion is why first-person narration is often favored in stories that explore themes of personal identity, self-discovery, or transformation.

Immediacy and Emotion in First-Person: One of the defining features of first-person narration is the immediacy it provides. The reader is placed directly in the character's shoes, experiencing the world and events in real time as the protagonist does. This proximity can enhance the emotional intensity of the story, making the reader feel the protagonist's fear, joy, confusion, or sadness in a direct and visceral way. This emotional immediacy is especially effective in building empathy for the character, drawing the reader into the narrative and fostering a sense of connection.

Reliability of Narrators in First-Person POV: The reliability of a first-person narrator is often questioned in stories where the character's perception of reality is distorted. This adds an element of uncertainty to the narrative. The reader must question the narrator's honesty, mental state, or emotional biases. In unreliable first-person stories like *The Tell-Tale Heart*, the narrator insists on their sanity despite evidence to the contrary, creating a tension between the reader's understanding of the truth and the narrator's conviction.

Emotionally Charged Narratives in First-Person: The first-person point of view lends itself well to stories that require an emotional punch. Since the narrative is filtered through the protagonist's emotions and perceptions, it is naturally more personal and emotionally charged. The reader feels as though they are experiencing the protagonist's inner turmoil firsthand, and this can create a more immersive and compelling emotional experience. This technique is often used in literary fiction, where deep emotional exploration is a central theme.

Revealing Character Secrets in First-Person: One of the fascinating aspects of first-person narration is how secrets are revealed. The narrator may hide crucial information from the reader at the beginning, only to reveal it later, creating dramatic tension. This withholding of information can serve as a form of suspense or mystery, as the reader is forced to piece together the truth through the narrator's actions and subtle hints. It also allows for dramatic irony, as the reader may know more than the narrator, leading to a deeper engagement with the plot.

Depth of Perception in Third-Person Limited POV: Third-person limited narration allows for a focused examination of a single character's thoughts, emotions, and perceptions. While the reader has access to this character's inner world, the narrative remains rooted in their perspective. This creates a sense of intimacy while maintaining some distance from the character, providing a balanced view of the character's internal and external experiences. This perspective works well in stories that focus on a protagonist's personal struggle or conflict, as it allows the reader to explore the character's complexities without overwhelming them with too much information.

Building Sympathy with Third-Person Limited: Third-person limited POV allows readers to empathize deeply with the protagonist while offering the narrative distance to observe their actions objectively. The narrative focuses on one character's experiences, but it does not fully immerse the reader in their subjective experience like first-person narration. This allows readers to form their own opinions about the protagonist's decisions and actions, which can lead to a more nuanced understanding of the character. As a result, the reader may develop a more complex form of sympathy or empathy for the character.

Restricting Knowledge in Third-Person Limited POV: One of the strengths of third-person limited narration is its ability to withhold information and build suspense. Since the story is filtered through the eyes of one character, the reader knows only what the protagonist knows. This restriction creates tension as the reader is kept in the dark about key details or plot developments, making for a more engaging and suspenseful narrative. As the story unfolds, the protagonist learns more about the world or other characters, which can provide the reader with new insights and plot twists.

Third-Person Limited POV and Emotional Focus: While third-person limited POV offers more objectivity than first-person, it still maintains a strong emotional focus on the protagonist. By exploring a character's emotions, thoughts, and reactions, the narrative provides insight into how the character processes the world around them. This emotional focus helps readers connect with the protagonist, even though they are not privy to the inner thoughts of other characters. The reader is guided to see the world through the protagonist's eyes, which can foster deep emotional engagement with the story.

Expanding Narrative Scope with Third-Person Omniscient: Third-person omniscient narration broadens the narrative scope by allowing the storyteller to move freely between different characters' perspectives. This narrative freedom provides a more expansive view of the story's world, allowing the reader to access not just the protagonist's emotions but also the inner workings of secondary characters. The omniscient narrator can also provide commentary on events and themes, offering insight into the broader world of the story. This technique is particularly effective in complex stories with multiple characters or intricate plots.

Omniscient Narration and Foreshadowing: An omniscient narrator has the unique ability to foreshadow events, providing the reader with hints about future plot developments or character decisions. By accessing the knowledge of all characters and the broader world, the narrator can drop subtle clues that create anticipation and tension. Foreshadowing in omniscient narration can also be used to create dramatic irony, where the reader knows more about what will happen than the characters do, heightening the emotional stakes.

Narrative Distance and Objectivity in Third-Person Omniscient: The third-person omniscient narrator offers a greater degree of objectivity compared to first-person or third-person limited narration. This objectivity allows the reader to see the characters and events from a wider perspective, without being emotionally tethered to one character's subjective experience. While this narrative distance can create a sense of detachment, it also provides clarity and a fuller understanding of the story, especially when multiple characters and subplots are involved.

Complexity of Character Relationships in Omniscient POV: In omniscient narration, the reader is privy to the thoughts and motivations of several characters, which allows for a more intricate exploration of relationships. The narrator can provide insight into each character's feelings toward others, revealing internal conflicts, hidden desires, and contradictions. This narrative flexibility enhances the complexity of character dynamics and allows the reader to see the story from multiple perspectives, deepening their understanding of the plot.

Exposing Themes and Symbolism in Third-Person Omniscient: Third-person omniscient narration is particularly effective at exposing themes and symbolism because the narrator has access to a wide range of information. The narrator can weave together different plot threads, motifs, and symbols to highlight deeper meanings that may not be immediately apparent to the characters themselves. By offering a more comprehensive view of the story's world, the omniscient narrator can underscore the thematic messages and symbols that give the story its resonance and significance.

CHAPTER 9

ESSAY WRITING

This chapter covers key essay writing strategies, focusing on structure, clarity, and argument development. It also explores Virginia Woolf's influence on the personal essay, highlighting her introspective style and narrative techniques to inspire effective and engaging writing.

A persuasive essay aims to convince the reader of a particular point of view or argument, often using logical reasoning and emotional appeal to influence the audience's beliefs or actions. The effectiveness of this type of essay hinges on the writer's ability to connect with readers on both intellectual and emotional levels.

The thesis statement in a persuasive essay serves as the backbone of the argument, clearly defining the position the writer takes on the issue at hand. A strong thesis not only states the writer's viewpoint but also hints at the evidence that will be used to support that position throughout the essay.

Logical reasoning is essential in persuasive essays, as arguments must be underpinned by facts, statistics, expert opinions, and other credible sources. This logical framework helps to solidify the argument and provides a foundation for persuading the reader.

Ethos, pathos, and logos are three rhetorical strategies commonly employed in persuasive writing. Ethos establishes the writer's credibility, pathos appeals to the reader's emotions, and logos relies on logical reasoning and evidence. A balanced use of these strategies can make the argument more compelling and relatable.

Effective persuasive essays proactively address counterarguments, acknowledging opposing views and providing rebuttals to strengthen the main argument. This demonstrates to readers that the writer has considered multiple perspectives and is prepared to defend their stance.

Transitions between paragraphs are crucial in persuasive essays, helping to maintain a coherent flow of ideas and reinforce the logical progression of the argument. Strong transitions guide readers smoothly from one point to the next, enhancing the overall readability of the essay.

Using anecdotes or examples in persuasive essays can enhance the argument by making it more relatable and concrete. Personal stories or real-world examples can evoke empathy and illustrate the broader implications of the argument, making it resonate with readers on a deeper level.

Virginia Woolf's essay "A Room of One's Own" exemplifies persuasive writing, as she uses personal narrative and social critique to advocate for women's rights to education and independence. Woolf's blend of storytelling and argumentation effectively persuades readers to consider the systemic barriers faced by women.

Research is crucial in persuasive essays to provide solid evidence that supports the argument and increases the essay's credibility. Well-researched essays not only bolster the writer's position but also demonstrate respect for the reader's intelligence by presenting substantiated claims.

Persuasive essays often appeal to the reader's emotions (pathos) through the use of vivid language, compelling imagery, and relatable scenarios. By engaging the reader's feelings, writers can create a connection that makes the argument more impactful.

A narrative essay tells a story, often from a personal perspective. It is structured to engage the reader emotionally and intellectually, presenting a series of events that convey a specific theme or lesson. This form of writing allows the writer to reflect on their experiences and share insights with the reader.

In narrative essays, the structure typically follows a clear progression: introduction (setting the scene), rising action (building tension), climax (the turning point), falling action (resolving conflicts), and conclusion (reflecting on the experience). This structure helps to create a compelling arc that keeps readers engaged.

Character development is key in narrative essays, even if the primary character is the author. Writers should create relatable, multi-dimensional characters that draw readers in and make them care about the outcomes of the story. Depth in characterization adds emotional weight to the narrative.

Descriptive language enhances narrative essays by immersing readers in the story, making the setting, characters, and events vivid and tangible. Effective descriptions evoke the senses, allowing readers to visualize and emotionally connect with the narrative.

A strong opening hook in a narrative essay captures the reader's attention immediately, often through an intriguing question, startling fact, or compelling anecdote. This hook encourages readers to continue reading, setting the tone for the rest of the essay.

The purpose of narrative essays is often to share an experience, convey a lesson, or illustrate a theme, but they also entertain and engage the reader through storytelling. A well-crafted narrative can provoke thought and inspire readers to reflect on their own experiences.

Virginia Woolf's novels, like Mrs. Dalloway and To the Lighthouse, showcase how narrative can blend with deeper analysis. Woolf's use of stream-of-consciousness allows for rich character exploration while still engaging readers in broader themes of time, memory, and identity.

A well-written narrative essay includes reflective elements, allowing the writer to analyze the significance of the events and their personal or broader impact. This reflection can provide insights that elevate the narrative from mere storytelling to a meaningful exploration of human experience.

First-person perspective is commonly used in narrative essays, providing an intimate, personal view of the events being described. This perspective fosters a sense of connection between the writer and the reader, as it shares not only what happened but also how it felt.

A narrative essay often relies on showing rather than telling, using vivid detail to convey the emotion and meaning behind the events. This approach allows readers to experience the story rather than simply hear about it, creating a more immersive reading experience.

Expository essays aim to explain or inform the reader about a specific topic or idea, relying on facts, statistics, and logical analysis. These essays are structured to present information in a clear and organized manner, making complex topics accessible to the reader.

An expository essay's thesis statement must clearly state the main topic or argument and outline the points that will be discussed. A well-defined thesis guides the direction of the essay and helps readers understand the focus of the writer's analysis.

Expository essays are structured with an introduction, body paragraphs (each focused on a specific point), and a conclusion that summarizes the key ideas. This structure enhances clarity and helps the reader follow the writer's line of reasoning.

Clear and concise language is essential in expository writing, as the goal is to inform rather than confuse. Avoiding jargon and overly complex sentences ensures that the content is accessible to a broad audience.

Virginia Woolf's essay "The Death of the Moth" serves as an exemplary model of expository writing, combining a simple observation about a moth's life with profound philosophical analysis. This blend allows readers to engage with both the narrative and the deeper reflections on life and death.

The body paragraphs in an expository essay should each focus on a single idea, introduced with a topic sentence and supported by evidence or examples. This clear organization helps readers understand and retain the information presented.

Analytical essays go beyond summarizing content; they break down a topic into its component parts, examining how they contribute to the whole. This type of essay requires critical thinking and the ability to interpret and evaluate various elements of the work being analyzed.

In an analytical essay, the writer evaluates how literary devices, rhetorical strategies, or arguments are used to achieve a particular effect or convey a message. This analysis provides insights into the deeper meanings and implications of the text.

Critical thinking is a vital skill in analytical essays, as the writer must interpret and evaluate the material rather than merely describing it. This ability to think critically enhances the quality of the analysis and encourages deeper engagement with the text.

Virginia Woolf's essays are often analytical, deconstructing social norms, literary conventions, and gender roles to offer deeper insight. Her work encourages readers to think critically about the structures of society and literature, often challenging traditional viewpoints.

The introduction of an essay must grab the reader's attention, often starting with a hook such as a quote, question, or surprising fact. A compelling introduction sets the stage for the argument or narrative that follows.

The conclusion of an essay should not just restate the thesis but also offer a final thought or call to action, leaving a lasting impression on the reader. A strong conclusion ties together the main points and emphasizes their significance.

Editing and revising are crucial steps in essay writing. Writers should focus on improving clarity, coherence, and flow while checking for grammar and spelling errors. This process can transform a rough draft into a polished final product.

Virginia Woolf was known for her stream-of-consciousness writing style, which, while primarily associated with fiction, also influenced her essay writing. This style allows for fluid, natural exploration of ideas, blending narrative with deep intellectual engagement.

Writers must consider their audience when crafting essays, adjusting tone, language, and argument complexity to fit the reader's knowledge and interests. Tailoring content to the audience enhances engagement and effectiveness.

Strong topic sentences at the beginning of each paragraph help guide the reader through the essay and clarify the argument being made. Clear topic sentences ensure that each paragraph contributes meaningfully to the overall thesis.

Essay writing requires a balance between analysis and evidence. Writers must interpret their evidence thoughtfully, connecting it back to the thesis while avoiding mere summary. This balance enriches the essay's argument and enhances its persuasive power.

Woolf's essays often explore social and cultural issues, offering both personal reflection and intellectual critique. This blend of narrative and analysis demonstrates the power of essays to engage with complex ideas while remaining accessible to readers.

Essay conclusions should reflect the broader implications of the argument or analysis, showing how the points discussed apply to larger issues. This helps readers see the relevance of the essay's topic in a wider context.

Effective essay writing involves a clear thesis, structured paragraphs, logical flow, and strong conclusions, all of which are exemplified in Virginia Woolf's essays, where narrative and deep thought seamlessly combine to create compelling and thought-provoking work.

CHAPTER 10

ARGUMENTATION AND DEBATE

Inspired by Frederick Douglass, this chapter highlights how his powerful speeches advanced abolition and civil rights, showcasing the impact of skilled debate.

A clear thesis statement is essential: A thesis statement provides the foundation for any persuasive speech or essay, clearly expressing the main argument in a concise way. Frederick Douglass excelled in delivering clear thesis statements, often opening his speeches with bold declarations that outlined his stance on abolition. This strategic choice immediately oriented his audience, giving them a clear understanding of his purpose and setting the stage for his argument. By establishing this clarity upfront, Douglass ensured his listeners stayed focused and engaged throughout his speech.

Logical reasoning supports your claims: Arguments grounded in logic and reason are more convincing because they appeal to the audience's intellect. Douglass masterfully employed logical reasoning by ensuring his conclusions naturally followed from his premises. He used coherent, step-by-step explanations to connect his points, making his arguments not only powerful but also irrefutable. This logical approach strengthened his credibility and appealed to those who valued rationality over emotional or biased appeals.

Understanding your audience is crucial: Persuasion becomes more effective when arguments are tailored to resonate with the audience's beliefs and values. Douglass demonstrated an acute understanding of his listeners, adapting his message depending on whether he was addressing abolitionists, skeptics, or undecided citizens. This sensitivity to his audience's perspectives allowed him to frame his arguments in ways that aligned with their priorities, increasing the likelihood that his message would be received favorably.

Using personal experience adds credibility: Sharing personal stories can humanize an argument and establish trust. Douglass's accounts of his life as an enslaved person brought a unique authenticity to his arguments, offering undeniable evidence of the injustices of slavery. These personal experiences allowed his audience to emotionally connect with his message, making his points more relatable and impactful.

Defining key terms clarifies your argument: Misunderstandings can undermine an argument, making it essential to define terms clearly. Douglass often explained critical concepts like "freedom" and "equality," ensuring that his audience understood these ideas as he intended. This clarity eliminated confusion and helped his listeners fully grasp the significance of his message, strengthening its overall impact.

Establishing common ground fosters connection: Finding shared values helps create a bond between the speaker and the audience. Douglass often highlighted universal ideals, such as justice and human dignity, to connect with listeners who might initially disagree with him. By appealing to these shared principles, he created a foundation of mutual understanding that opened the door to constructive dialogue.

Using a logical structure enhances clarity: A well-organized presentation helps audiences follow and remember arguments. Douglass structured his speeches with clear introductions, detailed bodies, and impactful conclusions. This logical flow built momentum, guiding listeners through his points and ensuring that his messages were both persuasive and easy to recall.

Addressing the significance of your argument: Explaining why an argument matters helps engage the audience on a deeper level. Douglass framed the abolition of slavery as a moral and universal issue, arguing that it was a fight for basic human rights that affected everyone. By emphasizing the broader implications of his cause, he made it clear that his arguments were not just relevant but essential.

Utilizing rhetorical questions engages the audience: Rhetorical questions encourage listeners to think critically about the topic.

Douglass frequently used this technique to challenge assumptions and provoke reflection. By posing thought-provoking questions, he inspired his audience to examine their own beliefs and consider the validity of his arguments more deeply.

Building emotional appeal can strengthen arguments: Emotional appeals can motivate audiences to act. Douglass skillfully evoked emotions such as empathy and outrage in his speeches, painting vivid pictures of the horrors of slavery. This emotional resonance not only captured his listeners' attention but also inspired them to support the abolitionist movement.

Incorporating credible evidence bolsters your argument: Evidence is the backbone of a strong argument, lending credibility and weight to claims. Frederick Douglass used historical facts, legal documents, and firsthand observations to support his stance on slavery. By citing concrete examples, such as specific laws or injustices, he reinforced his arguments and made them difficult to refute. This reliance on credible evidence showcased his thorough preparation and enhanced his persuasiveness.

Anticipating counterarguments shows thorough understanding: Acknowledging opposing views demonstrates not only confidence but also respect for the audience's intelligence. Douglass skillfully anticipated and addressed counterarguments in his speeches, often dismantling them before they were raised. This proactive approach highlighted his depth of understanding and his ability to engage in thoughtful, critical discourse, making his arguments more robust.

Refuting counterarguments enhances credibility: Providing well-reasoned rebuttals to counterarguments shows mastery of the subject. Douglass excelled at exposing the flaws and contradictions in opposing views, such as the justification of slavery based on economics or religion. By calmly and effectively dismantling these arguments, he strengthened his own position and gained the trust of his audience.

Using analogies can clarify complex points: Analogies help simplify abstract or difficult concepts by connecting them to familiar ideas. Douglass often used relatable comparisons to illustrate the injustices of slavery. For instance, he likened slavery to theft, emphasizing the moral wrong of depriving a person of their freedom. These analogies made his points more accessible and resonant.

Citing historical examples provides context: Historical references add depth and context to an argument, connecting it to broader narratives. Douglass frequently drew parallels between the abolitionist movement and events like the American Revolution, pointing out the hypocrisy of a nation founded on liberty yet tolerating slavery. These comparisons underscored his points and made his arguments more compelling.

Using expert opinions can enhance credibility: Quoting respected authorities strengthens arguments by associating them with established credibility. Douglass often referenced prominent abolitionists, intellectuals, and legal thinkers to support his views. This strategic use of expert opinions lent additional weight to his arguments and demonstrated that his stance was part of a larger, informed movement.

Employing visual aids can reinforce arguments: While Douglass primarily relied on powerful oratory, the modern application of this principle includes using visual aids like charts or slides to clarify and emphasize key points. Visual elements can engage audiences more effectively, making complex data or ideas easier to understand. If Douglass had access to such tools, he likely would have incorporated them to enhance his presentations.

Making data accessible is key: Presenting information in a clear and digestible manner ensures that the audience can grasp and retain it. Douglass excelled at breaking down complex societal issues into straightforward arguments that resonated with diverse audiences. His ability to simplify without losing depth exemplifies the importance of clarity in communication.

Addressing emotional responses respectfully is vital: Acknowledging and addressing emotional reactions to difficult topics helps maintain a constructive dialogue. Douglass understood the fears and anxieties of his audience, particularly those resistant to change. By showing empathy and speaking respectfully, he fostered a more open and productive conversation.

Using testimony from affected individuals adds authenticity: Personal stories bring an argument to life, grounding it in real experiences. Douglass's own narrative as a formerly enslaved person was one of his most powerful tools. By sharing his experiences, he offered irrefutable evidence of slavery's brutality, making his arguments both relatable and undeniable.

Understanding rhetorical strategies enhances persuasion: Effective arguments often employ a mix of ethos (credibility), pathos (emotion), and logos (logic). Douglass balanced these strategies masterfully, presenting himself as a credible speaker, appealing to the emotions of his audience, and using logical reasoning to support his claims. This combination made his speeches highly persuasive and impactful.

Using repetition can reinforce key points: Repetition emphasizes critical ideas, ensuring they resonate with the audience. Douglass often reiterated central themes, such as the moral imperative to end slavery, to drive home his message. This technique not only reinforced his points but also made his speeches more memorable.

Crafting compelling conclusions leaves a lasting impression: A strong closing statement ensures that the audience remembers the key takeaways. Douglass often ended his speeches with impassioned calls to action, urging his listeners to fight for justice and equality. These powerful conclusions inspired audiences and left a lasting impact.

Storytelling can enhance emotional engagement: Narratives captivate audiences by making abstract issues tangible and relatable. Douglass's speeches were often enriched with vivid stories and personal anecdotes, which drew his listeners in and made his arguments more emotionally resonant.

Establishing urgency can prompt action: Creating a sense of urgency motivates audiences to act rather than delay. Douglass emphasized the immediate need for abolition, arguing that the longer slavery persisted, the greater the harm to society. This urgency inspired many to join the abolitionist cause.

Using humor carefully can disarm opposition: Humor, when used appropriately, can lighten the mood and make difficult topics more approachable. Douglass occasionally employed wit and irony to engage his audience while maintaining respect for the seriousness of his subject matter.

Timing and pacing enhance delivery: A well-timed pause or change in pace can emphasize a point, give the audience time to reflect, or build anticipation. Frederick Douglass was skilled at modulating his voice and delivery to match the emotional tone of his speech. Whether delivering fiery condemnation or heartfelt appeals, his timing kept audiences engaged and added weight to his words.

Connecting personal stakes to broader issues adds depth: Douglass often connected his personal struggles to larger societal problems, framing his experience as a reflection of the systemic injustice of slavery. This approach personalized his arguments, making them relatable while highlighting the widespread nature of the issue.

Showing respect for diverse viewpoints builds rapport: Douglass frequently addressed audiences who held opposing views, including those who supported slavery. By approaching these situations with respect and addressing concerns directly, he built rapport and opened the door for meaningful dialogue. This strategy also demonstrated his confidence in his arguments.

Engaging the audience through rhetorical questions provokes thought: Douglass used rhetorical questions to challenge his audience's assumptions and provoke critical thinking. For example, he famously asked, "What, to the American slave, is your Fourth of July?" This question invited listeners to reflect on the hypocrisy of celebrating freedom in a nation that enslaved millions.

Emphasizing shared values fosters unity: Finding common ground with the audience helps to create a sense of unity and shared purpose. Douglass often appealed to universal values like liberty, justice, and humanity, showing how these ideals were incompatible with slavery. This approach made his arguments resonate with a wider audience.

Demonstrating authenticity earns trust: Douglass's passion and sincerity shone through in every speech, earning him the trust and respect of his audience. By speaking from the heart and staying true to his convictions, he created a powerful connection with listeners.

Addressing biases head-on challenges assumptions: Douglass did not shy away from confronting the biases of his audience, particularly those rooted in racism or ignorance. He exposed the flaws in their reasoning with logic and evidence, encouraging them to question and reconsider their beliefs.

Using concise language avoids confusion: While Douglass's speeches were eloquent, they were also clear and to the point. He avoided unnecessary complexity, ensuring that his message was accessible to all, regardless of their level of education.

Employing descriptive language creates vivid imagery: Douglass used descriptive language to paint vivid pictures of slavery's brutality. His ability to evoke powerful mental images made his speeches more impactful, allowing audiences to grasp the harsh realities he described.

Acknowledging progress inspires hope: While Douglass often highlighted the injustices of slavery, he also acknowledged progress where it had been made. This balance of critique and hope inspired audiences to believe that change was possible and motivated them to continue fighting for it.

Calling for collective action strengthens resolve: Douglass often reminded his audience that meaningful change required collective effort. By emphasizing the importance of unity and collaboration, he inspired individuals to work together toward the common goal of abolition.

Staying informed ensures relevance: Douglass was well-read and kept himself informed about current events, legal developments, and philosophical debates. This allowed him to address contemporary issues effectively and demonstrate his expertise.

Adapting to the audience enhances engagement: Douglass tailored his speeches to suit the audience, adjusting his tone, examples, and emphasis based on who he was addressing. This flexibility allowed him to connect with a diverse range of listeners, from rural farmers to urban intellectuals.

Demonstrating resilience inspires admiration: Douglass's own life story—overcoming slavery and becoming a leading intellectual and activist—was a testament to resilience. By embodying the values he advocated, he served as a powerful example and source of inspiration for his audience.

CHAPTER 11

CREDIBLE RESEARCH & ETHICAL WRITING: MLA, APA, AND PLAGIARISM PREVENTION

Inspired by Malcolm Gladwell's engaging use of research, this chapter show the importance of crafting ethical and compelling narratives.

A credible source is one that is trustworthy, reliable, and accurate. Credible sources are key to ensuring the validity of any argument or research. These sources can range from academic journals, expert interviews, historical documents, and statistical reports, all of which must be verified for their accuracy and legitimacy. Malcolm Gladwell often turns to such sources in books like *Outliers*, where he blends rigorous research with storytelling to strengthen his claims and make his arguments more compelling.

Peer-reviewed journals are some of the most credible sources because they are evaluated by experts in the field before publication. This evaluation process ensures that the research published is of high quality, relevant, and grounded in sound methodology. In his works, Gladwell frequently draws on peer-reviewed journals to substantiate his points, using these reputable sources to add depth and credibility to his analyses of human behavior, social dynamics, and psychology.

Books from established publishers are also considered reliable, especially those written by experts**.** Published books undergo rigorous editorial processes, ensuring that the content is fact-checked, well-researched, and professionally presented. Gladwell often references such authoritative texts in his own writing, reinforcing his arguments and establishing a solid foundation for his insights into complex subjects like societal trends and individual success.

Government reports and official statistics provide reliable data. These sources are typically based on large-scale studies and are created by governmental agencies, which are held to strict standards of accuracy and impartiality. Gladwell uses government data extensively in works like *The Tipping Point*, where he examines societal behaviors and the spread of trends using empirical evidence drawn from these trusted sources.

Expert interviews can enhance a source's credibility, especially when the expert is recognized in their field. By consulting individuals with deep knowledge and experience, Gladwell provides his readers with valuable insights from recognized authorities. These interviews help ground his storytelling in real-world expertise, giving his readers a more balanced and informed perspective on complex issues.

Newspaper and magazine articles can be credible if they come from reputable publications. Leading journals and respected media outlets, such as *The New Yorker*, where Gladwell himself has written, offer well-researched reporting and in-depth analyses. Gladwell often incorporates articles from these sources into his books, ensuring that his narratives are backed by trustworthy, well-sourced information.

University websites and educational institutions are credible sources for academic

research. These institutions are often at the forefront of academic studies, producing research and publications that are highly regarded in the academic community. Gladwell incorporates studies and findings from university-affiliated sources into his work to support his arguments and provide academic rigor to his analysis.

Be wary of sources with clear biases or opinions. Sources that exhibit strong ideological leanings or agendas may present distorted or one-sided views, which can undermine the objectivity of a research project. Gladwell is known for his careful selection of sources, ensuring that they present a balanced view and support his objective analysis rather than merely confirming preconceived notions.

When evaluating online sources, check the URL domain. Websites ending in .edu, .gov, or .org are typically more reliable because they are associated with educational institutions, government entities, or nonprofit organizations, all of which are generally trusted for factual, research-based information. Gladwell often refers to these types of websites in his research, ensuring that the data he presents is credible and sourced from reliable institutions.

Gladwell's research process demonstrates that finding multiple sources to corroborate facts is essential to avoid relying on a single, potentially biased source. By cross-referencing a variety of credible sources, Gladwell strengthens his arguments and provides readers with a comprehensive understanding of the topic at hand. This approach helps to ensure accuracy and avoid the pitfalls of relying on unverified or single-source information.

MLA format is typically used in humanities fields and involves in-text citations with the author's last name and page number. This format is crucial in academic writing as it allows readers to trace the origin of a specific idea or quote. In a literary analysis, for example, Gladwell's references would need to be formatted in MLA style to ensure that his citations adhere to academic standards.

APA format is commonly used in social sciences and includes the author's last name, publication year, and page number for in-text citations. This style is particularly useful when citing research in the fields of psychology, sociology, and education. Gladwell's works, which often delve into these subjects, could be cited using APA format for academic purposes, ensuring clarity and consistency in referencing.

In MLA format, the Works Cited page lists all sources alphabetically by the author's last name. This page serves as a comprehensive list of all the sources used in a work, making it easy for readers to locate the referenced material. Gladwell's books, which include a diverse range of sources, would follow this format to provide readers with a clear view of the research supporting his narrative.

In APA format, the References page includes the author's last name, first initial, publication year, title, and other relevant details. This organized structure helps readers identify the key information for each source and allows for easy tracking of the original materials used. Gladwell's extensive use of references would be formatted accordingly in APA style to maintain consistency and clarity.

Both MLA and APA formats require citing direct quotes and paraphrased ideas. Proper attribution is essential to ensure that intellectual property is respected. Gladwell's careful use of citations demonstrates how to ethically acknowledge the ideas of others while contributing original insights to the conversation.

Citing interviews in MLA requires listing the name of the person interviewed, the title of the interview (if applicable), the publication (if applicable), and the date. Gladwell frequently uses interviews in his work, and these would be properly cited in MLA format to maintain transparency and give due credit to the individuals whose perspectives contribute to his research.

APA citations for interviews would list the interviewee, interview date, and other pertinent details. This format ensures that interviews are cited correctly and provides readers with all necessary information to locate and verify the sources. Gladwell's frequent use of interviews would follow these guidelines, especially in his psychology-based works.

Gladwell often paraphrases the work of experts, but in an academic setting, such paraphrasing must still include proper in-text citation in both MLA and APA formats. Paraphrasing allows writers to present ideas in their own words, but it still requires acknowledgment of the original source. Gladwell's writing exemplifies how to incorporate expert insights while ensuring proper attribution.

Plagiarism occurs when a writer uses someone else's words or ideas without proper attribution. Plagiarism can damage a writer's credibility and reputation. Gladwell consistently avoids plagiarism by carefully crediting his sources, setting an example for other writers on the importance of academic honesty.

Paraphrasing involves rephrasing another person's ideas in your own words, but it still requires citation. Even when presenting ideas in a new form, proper citation ensures that the original source is credited. Gladwell's work often includes paraphrased material, but it is always attributed correctly, reflecting his commitment to ethical research practices.

Effective paraphrasing includes not only changing the words but also altering the structure of the original sentence. By transforming both the language and the structure of a sentence, writers can present complex ideas in a way that is easier for readers to understand. Gladwell excels in this skill, often reworking expert ideas into more accessible language while preserving their meaning.

Direct quotes should be used sparingly and require quotation marks. Quoting directly from a source helps emphasize key points and adds authority to a writer's arguments. Gladwell often uses direct quotes to underscore critical insights, ensuring that all quotes are properly attributed and punctuated.

Paraphrasing should be balanced with analysis. It's important to add personal interpretation to paraphrased material to provide context and deepen understanding. Gladwell masterfully blends paraphrased research with his own analysis, creating narratives that are both informative and thought-provoking.

Gladwell's work shows that when paraphrasing, it's important to add your voice and perspective rather than just rewording what the source said. Paraphrasing is an opportunity to reinterpret information, and Gladwell's writing reflects this by infusing his own insights into the research he presents.

Common knowledge does not require citation, but ideas specific to a source must be cited. Ideas that are widely accepted, such as basic scientific facts, can be presented without citation. However, Gladwell carefully cites studies and research findings that are not widely known to avoid misrepresenting sources.

Proper citation prevents plagiarism by showing exactly where information came from. By clearly citing his sources, Gladwell avoids the risk of plagiarism while also providing readers with a transparent view of his research process.

Turnitin and other plagiarism checkers are useful tools in academia to ensure originality. Tools like Turnitin help detect instances of plagiarism, providing an additional layer of integrity. Gladwell's thorough citations would pass such checks, highlighting the importance of proper source attribution.

Paraphrasing helps avoid plagiarism, but you still need to ensure that the original idea is clearly credited. Paraphrased content must be linked back to the source to avoid plagiarism. Gladwell demonstrates this through his consistent, transparent use of citations.

Gladwell's research process highlights the importance of checking facts. By cross-referencing multiple sources and presenting well-rounded perspectives, he ensures that his work is factually accurate and avoids relying on faulty or incomplete information.

CHAPTER 12

PUBLIC SPEAKING AND PRESENTATIONS

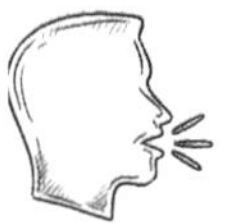

Discover timeless techniques inspired by Dr. Martin Luther King Jr. to craft compelling presentations, connect with audiences, and deliver impactful speeches. Learn to structure your message, use powerful rhetoric, and engage listeners with confidence and authenticity.

Understanding your audience is crucial when developing a presentation. Dr. King tailored his speeches to resonate with the diverse backgrounds of his listeners, ensuring his message connected deeply. For example, he considered their values, experiences, and expectations, allowing him to frame his arguments in a way that was relatable and compelling.

Establishing a clear purpose for your presentation helps guide content. King's speeches often focused on specific goals, such as advocating for civil rights or inspiring hope. This clarity enabled him to craft messages that were not only persuasive but also actionable, encouraging listeners to participate in the movement.

Creating a strong outline organizes ideas logically, facilitating easier comprehension. King meticulously structured his speeches, ensuring each point flowed smoothly into the next. A well-organized outline allows speakers to anticipate audience questions and address them proactively, enhancing overall engagement.

Incorporating storytelling can make presentations more relatable. King's use of personal anecdotes and historical references helped illustrate his points, making complex issues more accessible to his audience. By weaving stories into his rhetoric, he connected emotionally with listeners, making his message memorable.

Developing a compelling opening captures attention immediately. King famously started his "I Have a Dream" speech with a powerful vision, drawing listeners in from the very beginning. An impactful opening sets the tone for the entire presentation and can significantly influence audience engagement.

Using visual aids can enhance understanding. While King often relied on his words, modern speakers can benefit from slides, images, and videos to reinforce their message visually. Visual aids can simplify complex information and help retain audience interest.

Practicing delivery is essential for confidence. King rehearsed extensively, allowing him to deliver his speeches with passion and conviction, making them more impactful. Practice also helps speakers refine their timing, pacing, and body language, contributing to a more polished presentation.

Time management is critical in presentations. King understood the importance of pacing, ensuring he maintained audience attention without exceeding time limits. Effective time management allows speakers to cover all their material without rushing or dragging out points unnecessarily.

Incorporating audience interaction can foster engagement. King often encouraged participation, making his audience feel like an integral part of the movement he was advocating for. Techniques such as asking questions or inviting responses can create a more dynamic and inclusive atmosphere.

Ending with a strong conclusion reinforces the presentation's main message. King's speeches often culminated in a powerful call to action, leaving a lasting impression on his audience. A well-crafted conclusion summarizes key points and inspires listeners to take the next steps.

Understanding rhetorical devices can enhance speech effectiveness. King skillfully employed techniques such as repetition, as seen in his famous phrase "I have a dream," to emphasize key points. Rhetorical devices help to clarify messages and make them more persuasive.

Utilizing ethos, pathos, and logos strengthens arguments. King established credibility (ethos), appealed to emotions (pathos), and presented logical arguments (logos), making his speeches persuasive on multiple levels. This balanced approach engages listeners' hearts and minds, increasing the likelihood of acceptance.

Employing vivid imagery can paint a picture in the audience's mind. King used powerful imagery to evoke emotions, helping listeners visualize the struggles and hopes of the civil rights movement. Imagery can evoke strong feelings and create lasting memories of the presentation.

Creating contrasts can highlight key issues. King often juxtaposed the harsh realities of oppression with the vision of a just society, emphasizing the need for change. Contrasts can clarify complex issues and underscore the importance of addressing them.

Using rhetorical questions engages the audience and prompts them to think critically. King's speeches frequently posed questions that challenged listeners to reflect on their beliefs and actions, encouraging deeper engagement with the content.

Incorporating famous quotes can lend authority to your message. King quoted historical figures and religious texts, connecting his ideas to broader themes and principles. Citing reputable sources enhances credibility and demonstrates a well-rounded perspective.

Utilizing parallelism adds rhythm and memorability to speeches. King's repeated structure in phrases reinforced his messages and made them easier for the audience to remember. This technique also helps to build momentum throughout the speech.

Anecdotes and examples make abstract concepts concrete. King often shared stories of individuals affected by injustice, personalizing the struggle and fostering empathy. Real-life examples can humanize issues and make them more relatable to the audience.

Appealing to shared values helps create a bond with the audience. King invoked universal themes like justice and equality, uniting listeners around common beliefs. This connection can enhance persuasion by aligning the speaker's message with the audience's core principles.

Addressing counterarguments can strengthen credibility. King acknowledged opposing views while firmly rebutting them, demonstrating his understanding of the complexities surrounding civil rights. This approach shows respect for differing opinions while reinforcing the validity of his own arguments.

Maintaining eye contact fosters a connection with the audience. King's direct gaze engaged listeners, making them feel seen and heard. Eye contact helps build trust and rapport, making the audience more receptive to the message.

Vocal variety—altering tone, pitch, and volume—keeps speeches dynamic. King's passionate delivery conveyed urgency and emotion, enhancing the impact of his words. A varied vocal delivery can help maintain interest and emphasize key points.

Body language plays a significant role in communication. King's gestures and movements complemented his words, reinforcing his messages and demonstrating conviction. Effective body language can convey confidence and sincerity.

Pacing is key; speaking too fast can overwhelm listeners, while too slow may bore them. King's deliberate pacing allowed his powerful messages to resonate and be absorbed by the audience. A controlled pace enables audiences to follow along and digest information.

Using pauses strategically can emphasize key points. King's calculated pauses allowed his words to sink in, creating moments for reflection and impact. Pauses can also enhance the emotional weight of a message.

Eliminating filler words (like "um" and "uh") enhances professionalism. King's confident delivery demonstrated a mastery of language, free from distracting verbal tics. Clear speech reflects preparedness and authority.

Rehearsing in front of an audience can provide valuable feedback. King often practiced with trusted allies, refining his speeches based on their reactions and suggestions. Feedback helps identify areas for improvement and enhances overall delivery.

Adapting to the environment is essential. King delivered powerful speeches in various settings, adjusting his tone and approach based on the audience and context. Flexibility ensures that the message resonates regardless of the situation.

Encouraging audience participation can boost engagement. King often called on his listeners to join in solidarity, creating a powerful communal experience. Participation fosters a sense of belonging and commitment to the message.

Being authentic resonates with audiences. King's genuine passion for justice and equality shone through his speeches, making them relatable and inspiring. Authenticity creates a connection that encourages trust and loyalty.

Utilizing humor appropriately can lighten the mood. While King focused on serious issues, moments of levity helped balance the emotional weight of his message. Humor can make the speaker more relatable and engage the audience more effectively.

Staying composed under pressure is vital. King maintained his poise, even in charged situations, demonstrating confidence and credibility. Composure reassures the audience and reinforces the speaker's authority.

Adapting to feedback during delivery can improve the experience. King was responsive to his audience's reactions, adjusting his approach as necessary to maintain engagement. Being attuned to the audience helps address their needs in real-time.

Summarizing key points at the end reinforces the message. King often revisited main ideas, ensuring his audience left with a clear understanding of his vision. A summary helps solidify the message in the listeners' minds.

Using a consistent format for speeches can help audiences follow along. King's speeches often followed a familiar structure, making them easier to understand and remember. Consistency aids in audience comprehension.

Being mindful of time constraints is essential. King often tailored his speeches to fit the occasion, ensuring he delivered impactful messages within allotted timeframes. Respecting time shows professionalism and consideration for the audience.

Being aware of cultural sensitivities is crucial in public speaking. King navigated complex social issues with respect, emphasizing the importance of empathy and understanding. Cultural awareness fosters a positive reception and builds bridges with diverse audiences.

Creating a call to action motivates audiences to act. King's speeches often ended with a powerful call for change, urging listeners to join the fight for justice. A compelling call to action inspires commitment and mobilizes support.

Using personal conviction can inspire audiences. King's unwavering belief in his message galvanized support and motivated listeners to engage with the civil rights movement. Conviction is contagious; passionate speakers often ignite similar passion in their audiences.

Reflecting on past speeches can inform future presentations. King learned from his experiences, continuously evolving his speaking style to better connect with his audiences. Continuous improvement leads to greater effectiveness and impact over time.

CHAPTER 13

CREATIVE WRITING

This chapter explores key writing elements like narrative structure, vivid imagery, and character development, drawing inspiration from J.K. Rowling's works. It highlights the power of experimenting with genres, weaving universal themes, and refining stories through editing.

Understanding the structure of short stories: A typical short story consists of exposition (setting the scene), rising action (building tension), climax (the peak of conflict), falling action (leading to resolution), and resolution (conclusion). Rowling exemplifies this structure in her short works, where each element builds upon the last to create a satisfying narrative arc that captivates readers from start to finish.

Poetry relies on rhythm and meter: The musicality of poetry is achieved through rhythm (the pattern of sounds) and meter (the structured beats). Rowling's poetic elements in her writing often reflect emotional undertones, making the language resonate. For example, employing iambic pentameter can create a flow that enhances the overall impact of a poem.

Crafting a strong hook: The opening lines of a story are critical for capturing a reader's interest. Rowling often begins with intriguing scenarios or questions that prompt curiosity. A strong hook not only draws readers in but also sets the tone for the narrative, suggesting whether the story will be whimsical, serious, or thought-provoking.

Exploring themes: Themes provide the underlying message or insight of a narrative. In her works, Rowling explores universal themes like love, sacrifice, and friendship. By weaving these themes throughout her narratives, she connects with readers on a deeper emotional level, encouraging them to reflect on their own experiences.

Using vivid imagery: Descriptive language that appeals to the senses can create immersive experiences for readers. Rowling's detailed descriptions of settings, such as the magical atmosphere of Hogwarts, transport readers to fantastical realms, making them feel as if they are part of the story.

Writing with emotion: Infusing narratives with genuine emotion allows readers to connect with characters on a personal level. Rowling often portrays her characters' struggles and triumphs with sensitivity, evoking empathy and making their journeys relatable to readers of all ages.

Experimenting with different formats: Writers can explore various storytelling methods, such as flash fiction, prose poetry, or traditional narratives. By experimenting with format, Rowling can discover unique ways to express ideas, often resulting in creative breakthroughs and new ways of engaging with readers.

Editing is crucial for clarity and impact: The revision process is where writers refine their work. Rowling emphasizes the importance of editing her drafts to improve clarity, tighten prose, and ensure that every word serves a purpose. This meticulous process can significantly enhance the overall quality of the writing.

Creating relatable conflicts: Conflict drives a narrative and keeps readers engaged. Rowling constructs conflicts that reflect real-life challenges, such as identity struggles and moral dilemmas, allowing readers to see parts of their own lives in the characters' journeys.

Understanding the intended audience: Tailoring content to suit the audience helps ensure resonance. Rowling writes for children and adults alike, skillfully balancing humor, adventure, and poignant moments to engage diverse readers, making her work accessible and enjoyable for all ages.

Character development involves crafting backstories: A well-developed character has a rich history that informs their motivations and decisions. Rowling creates intricate backstories for her characters, which enhance their complexity and depth, making them feel like real people with relatable experiences.

Creating distinct voices for characters: Each character should have a unique way of speaking that reflects their personality, background, and emotional state. Rowling's ability to give each character their own voice—through specific word choices and speech patterns—helps to establish their individuality and makes them memorable.

Utilizing conflict to reveal character traits: Placing characters in challenging situations reveals their true nature. Rowling uses conflict strategically to show how her characters respond under pressure, allowing readers to witness their growth and develop a deeper understanding of their motivations.

Incorporating dialogue to advance the plot: Dialogue can reveal character relationships and propel the story forward. Rowling expertly uses conversations between characters to convey essential information, develop relationships, and maintain the narrative's momentum.**Using Subtext in dialogue:** Characters often communicate more than what is explicitly stated, adding layers to their interactions. Rowling employs subtext to create tension and complexity, allowing readers to read between the lines and engage with the characters' true feelings and intentions.

Creating ensemble casts: A diverse array of characters allows for rich interactions and dynamic storytelling. Rowling's ensemble cast in the Harry Potter series showcases a variety of personalities, perspectives, and backgrounds, enriching the narrative and providing multiple angles from which to view the story.

Balancing dialogue and narrative description: A harmonious blend of dialogue and description keeps readers engaged. Rowling intersperses dialogue with vivid descriptions of settings and emotions, creating a dynamic reading experience that immerses readers in the story's world.

Using humor can enhance character dynamics: Humor serves as a powerful tool to build relationships and diffuse tension. Rowling incorporates wit and clever banter among her characters, enhancing their interactions and making their relationships feel authentic and relatable.

Understanding character motivation drives the plot: Characters with clear goals propel the story forward. Rowling's characters are often driven by strong motivations—whether it's love, ambition, or the quest for justice—keeping readers invested in their journeys as they navigate obstacles to achieve their desires.

Experimenting with genres can inspire creativity: Engaging with various genres expands a writer's toolkit. Rowling's ability to blend fantasy with elements of adventure and mystery showcases how exploring different genres can lead to innovative and engaging storytelling.

Understanding genre conventions: Familiarity with established genre elements can provide a solid foundation for writing. Rowling's understanding of fantasy tropes enables her to play with reader expectations, subverting conventions to create fresh and unexpected narratives.

Mixing genres can create unique stories: Combining elements from different genres can lead to innovative storytelling. Rowling successfully merges fantasy with real-world themes, such as coming-of-age narratives, enhancing the relatability and depth of her stories.

Exploring themes across genres: Universal themes can transcend genre boundaries, creating connections between different works. Rowling's exploration of love, sacrifice, and friendship resonates across genres, allowing readers to find common ground in diverse stories.

Writing within established genres: Genre conventions provide structure and guidance for new writers. Rowling's foundation in fantasy offers a framework that allows her creativity to flourish while still appealing to genre enthusiasts.

Creating a unique voice within a genre: Developing a distinctive writing style helps a writer stand out. Rowling's blend of humor, vivid imagery, and engaging storytelling has carved a niche for her in the fantasy genre, attracting a devoted fan base.

Engaging with genre communities: Interactions with other writers and readers can foster support and inspiration. Rowling's connections within the fantasy writing community have provided her with valuable insights and encouragement throughout her career.

Reading widely in various genres: Exposure to different styles can enhance a writer's skills. Rowling's eclectic reading habits allow her to draw inspiration from various authors, enriching her own writing style and storytelling techniques.

Attending workshops or writing groups: Participating in collaborative environments can provide constructive feedback and support. Rowling's experiences sharing her work in writing groups helped refine her craft and build her confidence as a writer.

Creating sub-genres can inspire originality: Exploring niche categories within a genre can lead to fresh ideas. Rowling's fusion of fantasy with elements of mystery and adventure has led to a unique storytelling style that resonates with readers.

Utilizing different narrative styles: Experimenting with narrative perspectives can deepen storytelling. Rowling's use of third-person narration allows her to explore multiple character viewpoints, enriching the reader's understanding of the story's complexities.

Incorporating cultural elements: Drawing from cultural references can ground a story in authenticity. Rowling's use of folklore and myth enriches her world-building, creating a relatable context that resonates with readers from various backgrounds.

Using symbolism to add layers of meaning: Symbolism can enhance themes and character development. Rowling employs symbols, such as the Sorting Hat and the Patronus, to deepen the narrative and provide insight into characters' identities and struggles.

Exploring the relationship between genre and audience: Understanding audience preferences helps shape storytelling choices. Rowling's awareness of her readers allows her to craft narratives that resonate deeply, fostering connection and engagement.

Allowing room for experimentation: Embracing creativity can lead to new discoveries. Rowling's willingness to explore various ideas and styles has resulted in innovative storytelling that captivates her audience and defies traditional genre boundaries.

Establishing a writing routine: Consistency in writing fosters discipline and creativity. Rowling's dedication to daily writing not only enhances her skills but also helps maintain momentum and inspiration throughout the creative process.

Revisiting classic works: Engaging with literary classics can inspire innovation. Rowling's appreciation for classic authors such as C.S. Lewis and J.R.R. Tolkien has influenced her approach to fantasy writing and character development, enriching her own narratives.

Understanding genre expectations can enhance marketing: Aligning storytelling with genre conventions can aid in reaching target audiences. Rowling's success in the fantasy genre demonstrates the importance of marketing strategies that resonate with readers' interests.

Allowing room for experimentation encourages growth: Embracing creative risks can lead to significant breakthroughs. Rowling's willingness to take chances in her writing has fostered a dynamic and engaging narrative style that continues to evolve.

CHAPTER 14

LITERARY GENIUSES

This chapter examines literary geniuses—Ernest Hemingway, Edgar Allan Poe, Virginia Woolf, J.K. Rowling, and Jane Austen—each known for a distinct style and lasting impact. From Hemingway's minimalism to Rowling's fantasy worlds, their works showcase mastery in tone, structure, and character. Writers are encouraged to learn from their techniques to craft meaningful, enduring stories.

The Writing Process

Ernest Hemingway was known for his strict writing routine, often writing daily in a quiet, focused environment to facilitate creativity.

- Hemingway's revision process involved rewriting the same paragraph multiple times until he felt it captured his intent perfectly.

- He famously said, "The first draft of anything is crap," emphasizing the importance of revisions in crafting quality prose.

- Hemingway often published his works posthumously, revealing the depth of his ongoing revisions and improvements throughout his life.

Grammar and Sentence Structure

Jane Austen meticulously crafted her sentences, ensuring they were not only grammatically correct but also stylistically elegant.

- Austen's use of free indirect discourse blurred the lines between narration and characters' thoughts, showcasing her grammatical prowess.
- Her dialogue is often noted for its wit, illustrating her command of punctuation to enhance character voice and pacing.
- Jane Austen believed that clarity in sentence structure was essential for conveying her complex social commentary.

Vocabulary Development

William Shakespeare coined over 1,700 words, many of which are still in use today, showcasing his expansive vocabulary and creativity.

- He often used wordplay and puns, enriching his texts and demonstrating the power of context clues for meaning.

- Shakespeare's plays feature a variety of synonyms and antonyms, reflecting the richness of the English language and enhancing character development.

- His inventive use of language has influenced countless authors, demonstrating the importance of vocabulary in literary artistry.

Critical Reading and Comprehension

George Orwell employed clear, straightforward language in his works, allowing readers to grasp complex themes easily.

- His writing encourages close reading, prompting readers to analyze social commentary and biases in texts like *1984* and *Animal Farm*.

- Orwell's works highlight the importance of context and background knowledge for understanding nuanced arguments.
- He often employed satire to critique

- political ideologies, requiring readers to evaluate the arguments presented critically.

Literary Devices and Figurative Language

F. Scott Fitzgerald masterfully used symbolism, such as the green light in *The Great Gatsby*, to convey deeper meanings about the American Dream.

- His vivid imagery painted scenes that transported readers to the Jazz Age, illustrating the era's glamour and moral decay.

- Fitzgerald's use of irony often revealed the contradictions in society, particularly through character actions and societal expectations.

- His elegant prose style showcased the power of figurative language to evoke emotion and create lasting impressions on readers.

-

Analyzing Themes in Literature

Harper Lee explored the theme of racial injustice through the perspective of a child in *To Kill a Mockingbird*, making complex social issues accessible.

- The development of themes such as empathy and moral growth is intricately woven into the plot and character arcs in her novel.
- Lee's work encourages readers to confront their own biases and understand the implications of prejudice within society.
- The conflict between good and evil is central to the narrative, highlighting the struggle for justice in a flawed legal system.

Literary Analysis

Nathaniel Hawthorne's *The Scarlet Letter* serves as a key text for analyzing themes of sin, guilt, and redemption, making it a staple in literary studies.

- Hawthorne's use of symbolism, particularly the scarlet letter itself, invites deep analysis of character motivations and societal judgments.
- His writing style often blends historical context with psychological depth, allowing for multifaceted interpretations of his characters.
- The novel's complex narrative structure prompts discussions on moral ambiguity and the consequences of isolation.
-

Point of View and Perspective

Edgar Allan Poe is renowned for his use of unreliable narrators, compelling readers to question the truth of the narrator's account in stories like *The Tell-Tale Heart*.

- His exploration of first-person narration creates an intimate connection with the reader, drawing them into the psyche of his characters.
- Poe's distinct narrative voice often blurs the line between sanity and madness, encouraging readers to consider perspective critically.
- The shift in perspective within his tales highlights the subjectivity of truth, challenging conventional storytelling.

Essay Writing

Virginia Woolf combined narrative style with analytical depth in her essays, breaking traditional structures to explore complex ideas.

- Woolf's innovative use of stream-of-consciousness allowed her to weave personal reflections into broader societal critiques.

- Her essays often highlight the importance of the individual voice, encouraging writers to infuse personal experiences into their narratives.

- Woolf's meticulous attention to detail and form exemplifies the art of crafting engaging, thought-provoking essays.

Argumentation and Debate

Frederick Douglass utilized powerful rhetoric in his speeches to advocate for abolition, effectively employing emotional appeals and logical reasoning.

- Douglass's ability to address counterarguments made his case for civil rights compelling, demonstrating the importance of understanding opposing views.
- His speeches often featured vivid anecdotes that illustrated the human cost of slavery, reinforcing his arguments through emotional resonance.
- Douglass's insistence on the moral imperative of abolition galvanized support and fostered dialogue around civil rights issues.

Research Skills

Malcolm Gladwell seamlessly integrates research findings into his nonfiction writing, illustrating the importance of credible sources in storytelling.

- Gladwell's use of statistical data alongside personal anecdotes enriches his narratives and enhances their persuasive power.

- He emphasizes the significance of critical thinking in evaluating sources, encouraging readers to seek out reliable information.

- Gladwell's engaging writing style demonstrates how research can be woven into compelling narratives, making complex ideas accessible.

Creative Writing

J.K. Rowling created immersive worlds in the *Harry Potter* series, showcasing the importance of detailed world-building in fiction.

- Rowling's characters are rich and relatable, reflecting her skill in developing dialogue that reveals personality and depth.

- Her narrative structure often intertwines various genres, from fantasy to coming-of-age, highlighting the versatility of creative writing.

- Rowling's use of themes such as friendship, courage, and identity resonates with readers of all ages, making her work universally appealing.

Creative Writing

Stephenie Meyer's *Twilight* series is a rich exploration of emotional depth, narrative voice, and classic literary themes reimagined through a supernatural lens. Her first-person storytelling immerses readers in Bella Swan's internal world, highlighting themes of identity, longing, and transformation. Each installment draws inspiration from classic literature:

- *Twilight* mirrors *Romeo and Juliet* with its theme of forbidden love.

- *New Moon* echoes the heartbreak of *Wuthering Heights*, portraying loss and longing.

- *Eclipse* explores choice and loyalty like *Pride and Prejudice*.

- *Breaking Dawn* delves into transformation and sacrifice, reminiscent of *The Metamorphosis*.

About The Author

We believes in the lifelong *pursuit of knowledge* and the power of learning to transform lives.
With a deep passion for discovery and a commitment to sharing that passion, we encourages readers to view *education* as a continuous journey. This book is a testament to that belief, offering insights and inspiration for those who seek to *expand their understanding* of the world around them. By embracing curiosity and *never ceasing to learn*, we can all grow, innovate, and make lasting contributions to society.

www.ingramcontent.com/pod-product-compliance
Ingram Content Group UK Ltd.
Pitfield, Milton Keynes, MK11 3LW, UK
UKHW041820200726
13854UKWH00001BA/9

9 781958 189481